*Bismillah,
live every mome
as if it is y*

Imagine
that
Today is Your
Last Day

How would you act if you knew that
today was the last day of your life?

Zohra Sarwari

Eman Publishing
P.O. Box 404
FISHERS, IN 46038
USA

www.emanpublishing.com

Order Online: www.zohrasarwari.com

ISBN 13: 978-0-9823125-1-3
ISBN 10: 0-9823125-1-2
LCCN: 2009901038

EMAN
publishing

Cover Design by Zeeshan Shaikh

Printed in the United States of America

Imagine that Today is Your Last Day

How would you act if you knew that today was the last day of your life?

Zohra Sarwari

Dedication

'(Our Lord! Accept this from us; You are the All-Hearing, the All-Knowing).'

(The Qur'aan: Chapter 2, Verse 127)

Acknowledgements

In the name of the Allaah, the Most Gracious, the Most Magnificent. All praise is due to Allaah, Lord of the universe. We praise Him, and seek His help and His forgiveness, and we seek His protection from the accursed Satan. Whomever Allaah guides will never be misguided, and whomever He allows to be misguided will never be guided. I bear witness that there is no deity worthy of worship except Allaah, who is One, alone, and has no partners. I bear witness that Muhammad is His servant and messenger. May the blessings of Allaah be upon him and his family and his companions and the righteous who follow them until the Day of Judgment.

I would like to thank my family and friends for all of their support, especially Zeeshan, Madeeha, and Saqib Sheikh, who are an asset to my team   masha'Allaah. A very special thanks goes to Dr. Daoud Nassimi for all of his efforts and hard work in editing this book - jazaakAllaahu khayran! May Allaah (SWT) reward you all -   ameen!

Terminology

1. **"ALLAAH"** is the Arabic name for 'THE ONE SUPREME UNIVERSAL GOD'.
2. **"SWT"** is an abbreviation of the Arabic words **"Subhaanahu wa Ta'aalaa"** that mean **"Glory Be To Him."**
3. **Al-Qur'aan:** The Book of Allaah. A divine guidance for mankind. The FINAL TESTAMENT.
4. **Muslim** is one who has submitted to the Will of ALLAAH.
5. **Allaahu-Akbar** means 'Allaah is the Greatest'.
6. **Assalaamu 'alaykum** means 'Peace be on you.' This is a greeting for Muslims. The response to this greeting is 'Wa 'alaykum assalaam,' which means 'And Peace be upon you.
7. **Hajj** is one of the five pillars of Islam, a duty one must perform during one's life-time if one has the financial resources for it. It must be performed during certain specified dates of Dhul—Hijjah (the twelfth month in the Islamic calendar).
8. **PBUH** means Peace be upon him.
9. **PBUT** means Peace be upon them.
10. **Alhamdulillaah** means 'Praise is for God!'
11. **JazaakAllaahu khayran** means 'May Allaah rewards you with good.'
12. **5 Daily Prayers: 1. Fajr** (pre-dawn): This prayer starts off the day with the remembrance of Allaah (SWT); it is performed before sunrise. **2. *Dhuhr*** (noon): After the day's work has begun, one breaks shortly after noon to again remember Allaah (SWT) and seek His guidance. **3. *'Asr*** (afternoon): In the late afternoon, people are usually busy wrapping up the day's work, getting kids home from school, etc. It is an important time to take a few minutes to remember Allaah (SWT) and the greater meaning of our lives. **4. *Maghrib*** (sunset): Just after the sun goes down, Muslims remember Allaah (SWT) again as the day begins to come to a close. **5. *'Isha***

(evening): Before retiring for the night, Muslims again take time to remember Allaah's (SWT) Presence, Guidance, Mercy, and Forgiveness.

13. **Adhaan** is the call to prayer
14. **Du'aa** is supplication in Islam.
15. **Astaghfirullaah** means 'I seek forgiveness of Allaah.'
16. **Insha'Allaah** means 'if Allaah wills'.
17. **Shahaadah** means "I bear witness that there is no deity (none truly to be worshipped) but, Allaah, and I bear witness that Muhammad is the messenger of Allaah."
18. **Jamaa'ah** means congregation.
19. **Janaazah** means the funeral of a Muslim.
20. **Masjid** means mosque.
21. **Halaqah** literally means a ring or a circle. When used in Islamic terms it relates to 'circles of knowledge.'
22. **Imam** means guide.
23. **Aayah** means a verse in Qura'an.
24. **Ahadith** is the plural of hadith. Hadith means the actions and sayings of Prophet Muhammad (PBUH), reported by his companions and collected by scholars who came after them in books.
25. **Jannah** means Paradise.
26. **Ihraam** is the state of purity required of Muslim pilgrims before conducting the pilgrimage in Makkah.
27. **Qiblah** means the direction of the prayer, which is towards the Ka'bah in Makkah. Muslims all around the world are required to turn in this direction when praying.
28. **Rukoo** is to make a bow during pray.
29. **Sujood** is prostration to God that is usually performed during prayer.
30. **Musallaa** is the area designated for prayer.
31. **Masha'Allaah** means "It is what Allaah willed.'
32. **Halaal** means anything that is permissible under Islamic law.
33. **Tahajjud** is a voluntary prayer read in the last part of the night. It is also known as 'qiyaam.'

34. **Subhaan'Allaah** means "Glory to Allaah".
35. **Takbeer** is the saying of 'Allaahu Akbar.'
36. **Sunnah** means the deeds, sayings and approvals of Muhammad (PBUH).
37. **Sahaabah** means Companions of the Prophet Muhammad (PBUH).
38. **Deen** means Religion.
39. **Dunya** means the world.
40. **(RA)** stands for *Radiya 'Llaahu 'anhu,* which means "May Allaah be pleased with him."
41. **Surah** means a chapter in Qur'aan.
42. **Aakhirah** means 'The Hereafter' or the life of the next world
43. **Hijaab** refers to the women's dress code.
44. **Muslimah** is the word used for a Muslim woman.
45. **Al-Barzakh** is the realm after death in Islam.
46. **Zakaah** means 'purification' and 'growth'. It is the compulsory charity.
47. **Hijrah** means emigration.
48. **Tasleem** salutation of peace.
49. **Wudhu** means ablution.

Table of Contents

Chapter

1

Accepting Death

"Winning is not a sometime thing; it's an all the time thing. You don't win once in a while; you don't do things right once in a while; you do them right all the time. Winning is a habit. Unfortunately, so is losing."
-Vince Lombardi

"Wow!" Zeba said, "I can't believe how fast things are going. I feel that it has been weeks, and yet it has been months since we sold our talking interactive computer to Microsoft." Wali and their parents smiled.

Grandma looked up and said, "It feels like such a big load has been taken off our shoulders alhamdulillaah! Yet now we have the burden of ensuring we spend this money the correct way, for the sake of Allaah (SWT)." Everyone was looking at Grandma, and definitely felt the burden of the money. Yet, they had high hopes for what they wanted to accomplish. Wali and Zeba knew that this was a big test and they knew what they needed to do.

Their mother was looking at her husband and said quietly, "I am worried about these kids. What if they misuse the money, or spend it inappropriately? How will they answer for it on the Day of Judgment? How will we answer for it?"

Her husband listened attentively to every word she had said. His heart sank as he looked down and said, "This is all from Allaah (SWT), and insha'Allaah He will guide them to do what's right. Everything is from Allaah (SWT), and He has guided them this far, and has showered them with good manners, and given them this opportunity. Insha'Allaah, I have full tawwakal (confidence) in Allaah (SWT) that He will guide them, and us. Remember, our kids don't do anything without asking us first." As he said those last words, he smiled, yet, only Allaah (SWT) knew what he felt in his heart . . .

Two weeks had gone by, and Zeba and Wali's finals were finally over. Wali knew that it was time to set up what they had discussed. He arranged to meet up with Zeba in the morning after Fajr prayer. "Zeba, I want to start off by *going to the bank with dad, and opening up an account to put our money in. I want you to work with the attorney that Uncle Zakariya recommended to us. He is awaiting our phone call to set up the corporation and non-profits that we plan on working on, insha'Allaah. I also want you to get a list of all the non-profits that we want to donate to. Next, I want you to find out exactly when Hajj falls this year. I believe it will be in 3 months, since Ramadhaan is around the corner." Zeba was writing everything he was saying. She was so excited.*

Zeba looked up; smiled and said, "Wali, all this feels like a dream come true. SubhaanAllaah, I still can't believe it!"

Wali smiled back, and said, "Alhamdulillaah". They each went their separate ways to begin their to-do lists.

As Zeba was making her phone call, her mother came in; "Zeba, I want to talk to you about something."

Zeba hung up the phone as it just began dialing out. "Yes, Mom, is something bothering you? You seemed kind of quiet this morning."

Her mom looked at her with tears in her eyes and said, "Your cousin Rashad has been in a terrible car accident as he was going to school this morning. He is in hospital right now. The doctors don't think he will survive." By now she was sobbing, and Zeba was crying too. She hugged her mother, and was baffled by the news. She didn't know what to think or how to react; she was crying because her mother was crying. All she could think of was how two weeks ago all of them were together, talking about their plans and their life ahead of them. Zeba and Wali spoke about death with their parents and grandparents often, but it was still hard to digest that it can happen to someone young. "Zeba, are you okay?"

Zeba looked up and said "Yes, Mom. When will we go to see Rashad and Uncle Zakariya's family? I want to be there to help out with anything I can."

Her mom smiled through her tears; she wanted the same thing, "I spoke to your dad, and as soon as they return, we will all head out to Carmel. I need you to help me right now to prepare some food for everyone to take over there. I also need you to help pack some clothes for the next few days for Grandma, and yourself. We will stay there until we know what happens insh'Allaah"

Zeba, trying to keep her tears inside rushed to her room and grabbed a few long dresses and scarves to match. She tried to put them away neatly in her suitcase. Tears started rolling down her face. She kept telling herself that everything will be okay insha'Allaah: "I can't think of the worst-case scenario when it hasn't even happened. I have to get a hold of myself," she murmured to herself. She then began reciting some verses from the Qur'aan; that always calmed her down. She was at peace as she recited them and contemplated on their meaning. Soon after, she was knocking on Grandma's door, and Grandma was just picking up Grandfather's clothes. "Bebe jaan (Grandma dearest), I am here to help get your suitcase together."

Her grandma looked at her sadly and said, "So I guess you heard the news?" Zeba nodded her head and began pulling some of Grandma's dresses off the hangers. She folded them and began to put them in the suitcase; she knew which dresses her grandma liked. Grandma loved the fact that Zeba took initiative in all that she did. They were both silent throughout the packing; each in their own thoughts.

"Zeba, are you packed?" Mom called.

"Yes, Mom, I am. Grandma's almost done as well. We will be done in just a few minutes, insha'Allaah." Minutes later they were downstairs. Mom was just done with preparing the meat, and water was boiling on the stove for the rice. Zeba knew what she needed to do; her mother had taught her how to cook, and Zeba knew it was time to just act, not ask. She noticed the water boiling, and decided to dump the rice in the water. As she was cooking the rice, her mom was making the stew. Grandma sat at the table and began peeling potatoes. Everyone was chipping in to get things done faster. Moments later the men arrived home. Everyone was silent, and just wanted to get to the hospital as soon as they could.

"I'll drive," said Wali.

His dad looked at him as he had only been driving for a few months, and said, "It's a long drive, son, maybe I should do it."

"I just want you to relax, Dad; I have the navigation system in the car to direct me. Just relax, and I will ask you if I need help." Mom agreed. Everyone got into the minivan, and Wali began driving. The whole ride they were listening to the recitation of the Qur'aan on CD. Everyone was in a state of peace, pondering over the meaning that was recited afterwards. Everyone was in their own world, thinking about what was happening.

Finally, Grandma said, "When we get there Rashad might look distorted due to the car accident. Everyone pay attention to the expressions on your faces. Please don't show him anything that will make him know. Just be short and sweet when you're talking to him." Those were the last words said during the journey . . . everyone nodded.

"Excuse me, where is room 202A?" Wali asked.

"Go straight down, make a right at the end of the hallway, and then take the elevator to the 2nd floor," said the bubbly nurse. She wasn't smiling now, because she saw that everyone looked serious, and the 2nd floor was for ICU patients. Everyone's heart was beating 1000 beats an hour, and just being in the hospital made them feel anxious.

"Mom, you have to control your tears," Zeba said, as she saw tears coming down her mom's face.

"I can't help myself . . . he is my eldest nephew. I was there when he was born. I was there to hold him, and he used to sleep next to me whenever he came over. I love him as I love Wali." Mom was thinking about when Rashad was born, and how she was pregnant with Wali at that time. She loved Rashad and only wanted the best for him, to see him hurt was as if she saw Wali hurt.

"Uncle Zakariya is over there in the waiting area," Wali pointed. They all walked over to Uncle Zakariya, who had his head down and was making dhikr.

"Assalamu-alaykum wa rahmat-Ullaahi wa barakatuhu," said Wali's dad. Uncle Zakariya jumped onto his feet and greeted them. He couldn't help the tears that were flowing down his face. After greeting everyone, he went to his sister. They both just cried thinking about the situation they were in. He loved his sister, and knew she understood more than anyone. Uncle Zakariya and Mom were only two years apart, and they were the best of friends while growing up.

"Can we see him?" said Mother.

Uncle Zakariya nodded, "Yes, only two people at a time. You have to talk very softly. He has only been out of surgery for a few hours. He is in and out of consciousness. Grandma and Grandpa, will you do the honors?" Mother and Father looked at Grandma and Grandpa for they were the eldest. They nodded, and walked besides Uncle Zakariya; they were both reciting verses from the Qur'aan, and could feel a heavy weight on their shoulders as they walked into the room.

"Assalamu-alaykum, Rashad," said Grandpa. Rashad opened his eyes slightly and tried to reply. "Son, I know you can hear us but you can't really talk. In your heart recite the Qur'aan as much as you can, and Grandma and I will be doing the same. You know that only Allaah (SWT) can heal you. You need to be remembering Him and asking for forgiveness as much as you can. We love you and will be here for you, insha'Allaah." Grandma knew that was the best advice for him, she also kept reciting verses from the Qur'aan and had tears in her eyes as she watched him so weak, and with so many bruises on his face and body. She almost didn't recognize him. Grandma went over to him, and told him to say the Kalimah- Laa 'ilaaha 'illallaah (There is none worthy of worship but Allaah). She then said it with him, as he said the Shahaadah. Grandma kissed him on the forehead, and smiled through her tears.

"I need everyone out, I have to change his catheter bag," said the nurse. He knew that the family only wanted a male nurse to take care of Rashad's personal needs. The three of them told Rashad they would be back shortly insha'Allaah, and for him to just keep reciting as much of the Qur'aan as he could.

As they stepped out of the room, Wali rushed over, "Grandma, how was he?"

"He is in a very bad condition. He needs everyone's prayers at this time." It was then that Zeba looked at her watch and noticed it was time to pray 'Asr.

"Let's go and pray 'Asr in jamaa'ah," Zeba said. Everyone agreed, and went to the restroom to make ablution (wudhu). Ten minutes later everyone was in the waiting area, spreading their prayer rugs to pray. Zeba's father was leading the prayer as he had memorized the most Qur'aan. "Mom, why was Father crying when he was reciting today?" Zeba asked. Mom had tears in her own eyes, and just stayed silent. In a way Zeba knew the reason, but she wanted to see what answer her mom gave. Zeba knew it was time to stay quiet and that her mom would explain it later insha'Allaah. Moments after they finished praying, Uncle Zakariya's wife Khadijah, and their daughters, Fatima and Sarah came in; everyone greeted each other, exchanging tears. Fatima was just a bit older than Zeba; almost one year. Fatima was born right after Rashad, whereas Zeba was born two years after Wali. The girls looked at each other, and knew that this was serious stuff. Fatima was very close to Rashad. Sarah was the youngest, and was only seven years old; she didn't know how to react, she just watched everyone else, and sat by Grandma, holding onto her hand.

"Wali, Zeba! Please go bring the food from the car," their Mother called.

"Wali, what do you think will happen to Rashad? Will he be okay?" Zeba asked, as they hurried towards the car.

"I don't know. Only Allaah (SWT) knows. All we can do is pray for him. Just make du'aa for whatever is best for him . . . make du'aa that his pain is lessened," Wali said, as he handed two bags of food to Zeba to take in. On their way back both Wali and Zeba were quiet in their own thoughts.

"Let's set up the food in the sitting area, buffet- style, and then we will ask everyone to help themselves," Mother said. You could see the sadness in her face, and yet she had to be strong in order to take care of the needs of others. There was no time to waste worrying about her feelings. Zeba was paying attention to the details of what *was happening and how everyone was dealing with it. She looked at everyone for their strength. "Zeba, take the rice over there, and bring me the vegetarian dish," her mother said, interrupting Zeba's thoughts. Zeba hurried to do as her mother asked. Everyone recited some more verses from the Qur'aan as they sat there, and tried to comfort one another with the words of Allaah (SWT). Even Zeba and her mother were reciting as they were organizing the food. This was the state they were most comfortable in. "Dinner is served, please come and eat," Mother said. Father then asked Grandpa to lead the way because he was the eldest.*

"Let's eat, and then we will pray Maghrib together, insha'Allaah," Grandpa said, as he got up. Everyone just followed Grandpa; they all waited for their turn . . . no one was in a rush to eat.

"Khadijah, why aren't you eating?" Grandma asked.

Khadijah just smiled as a tear came down her face, and replied, "I'm not hungry. All I want to do is recite Qur'aan, and pray for his wellbeing."

Grandma stopped eating, and moved to sit next to Khadijah. She held her hand, and said, "You know the outcome will be as Allaah (SWT) has decreed for it to be. All we can do is make supplication to Allaah (SWT). I want you to be ready for the worst-case scenario, and know that everything is from Allaah (SWT), and that Allaah knows best. Please eat something, and let Allaah (SWT) guide us to the path He has decreed for us." Khadijah realized she was right; there was nothing she could do and things would be as Allaah (SWT) had willed. She would have to accept things as they were. Khadijah began picking at her food; she forced herself to eat whatever she could.

"Zakariya?! I need to speak to Zakariya or Khadijah," the doctor said, as he took off the mask from his face.

"I am Zakariya," Uncle Zakariya replied as he jumped onto his feet. Khadijah got up as well, but didn't say a word.

"May I speak to both of you alone?" the doctor asked. They both looked at each other a bit worried, but knew that whatever the outcome was, it was from Allaah (SWT). "Rashad, as you know has been in a terrible car

accident, he has been under major surgery, and was in a coma for hours. I am sorry to be the one to tell you this, but Rashad just took his last breath. We did everything we could." the doctor told them. Khadijah just looked at Zakariya as tears were streaming down her face.

"Innaa lillaahi wa innaa ilayhi raaji'oon. (To Allaah we belong and to Allaah we return)," Uncle Zakariya said to Khadijah. She repeated it. Everyone then came up and said it to Uncle Zakariya and Aunt Khadijah. Everyone had tears in their eyes as they were saying this. Yet they knew to expect the worst-case scenario. All of a sudden Fatima and Sarah understood; they had been talking to Zeba in a corner, and hadn't seen the doctor come.

"Zeba, Fatima, Sarah, there is some bad news we have to tell you," Zeba's mom called.

"What is it, Mom?" Zeba asked.

"Your cousin, Rashad just passed away," her mother said.

"What?!" screamed Fatima. Sarah and Fatima ran to their mom and dad, "Is it true Mom? Tell me they made a mistake. Tell me they're just kidding, and he is going to be okay. Tell me!" Fatima shrieked.

""Innaa lillaahi wa innaa ilayhi raaji'oon (To Allaah we belong and to Allaah we return)," said Uncle Zakariya, through his tears. He just hugged both of his daughters. Khadijah just cried, and excused herself to call her family. She was shaken but she knew that everyone was waiting to hear about this.

"I will go and see Rashad," said Uncle Zakariya.

"I will go with you," said Grandpa. Both men were silent on the walk over there, except tears now flowed down Uncle Zakariya's face.

"If you two will follow me please," said the nurse. Every step to the room made Zakariya feel like he could no longer hold his emotions, he just cried quietly as he looked at his son. He covered his face. All he could do was make supplication.

"We need to get the body to the funeral home to wash, and get ready for the janaazah," Grandpa said.

"I just called the masjid, and they said they will be ready to take the body when it is sent to them," Father said, stepping into the room as Uncle Zakariya was filling out the paperwork to move the body to the masjid.

It felt like hours as everyone was thinking of tomorrow, and how they would go through this process. More than anything, everyone was worried about Rashad's transition into the next life. That night everyone just recited Qur'aan, prayed, and supplicated for Rashad's forgiveness, and for his transition into the grave.

"Mom, what happens on your first night in the grave?" Zeba asked.

"Oh, Zeba! There is so much to tell you. Let me talk to your father and see if he can ask the Imam who is here right now, to give a halaqah on this topic for everyone to listen to. Since this is the first death that you are experiencing, it is a good time to have a better understanding of the whole process."

"Jazaak Allaahu khayran, Mom," Zeba said. Mom hurried off to the other room where Father was, and talked to him.

"I wonder if tonight will be the night we find out about the whole process with a dead person," Sarah said. Zeba and Fatima looked at Sarah and they too wondered the same thing. What seemed like hours, was only minutes away.

"The Imam has agreed to give an hour lecture on the process of dying and what happens once we enter the next world. I want all of you to remember that this can be a scary event. However, it is the truth, and the truth should be known," Mom announced. Everyone just nodded. A few minutes later, Wali, Dad, Grandpa, Uncle Zakariya, Aunt Khadija, and Grandma all entered the living room. Everyone was quiet and the Imam had the Qur'aan and some notes in his hands. The men sat towards one side, while the women were sitting on the other side and got comfortable and Zeba sat closer to Grandma. The Imam looked over some notes while everyone just waited patiently. No one was in the mood to talk, and everyone wanted to hear tonight's information.

"I want to read an ayaah from the Qur'aan at this time," the Imam said:

"And a soul will not die but with the permission of Allaah, the term is fixed; and whoever desires the reward of this world, I shall give him of it, and whoever desires the reward of the hereafter I shall give him of it, and I will reward the grateful." (The Qur'aan 3:145)

"To Him belongs the dominion of the heavens and the earth: It is He Who gives life and death; and He has power over all things."
(The Qur'aan 57:2).

"Okay, I will start with the actual rituals, and then go into detail as to what happens in the grave. What I will talk about is something serious, and we all should be aware of it, as anyone of us could be next. No one would have thought Rashad would have gone before us. Life is so unpredictable that we must be ready at all times for death insha'Allaah.

"First of all, when one is dying he/she should be encouraged to say the Shahaadah- 'Laa ilaaha illallaah – there is no (other) god except Allaah.' This is important to say before one dies, as the Prophet (PBUH) said: 'Prompt your dying ones to say "Laa ilaaha illallaah".

"Now, in the current situation of Rashad, alhamdulillaah your grandmother said it with him, may Allaah (SWT) accept it from him-ameen!

"After the individual has passed away we must close his/her eyes, for the Prophet (PBUH) said:

"When the soul is taken, the eyesight follows it."
(Muslim, Ahmad)

"Also, the entire body of the deceased should be covered with a sheet of cloth, except for the one who dies in a state of Ihraam - that is, whilst performing Hajj or 'Umrah, in which case the head and face should not be covered (Bukhari, Muslim).

"We must remember that we must pay off the debt of the deceased from any wealth he has left behind, and if he has no wealth then his closest relatives and other Muslims are encouraged to pay for him (Ahmad, al-Hakim, and others. Verified to be hasan by al-haythami and al-Albani (Ahkaam ul-Janaa'iz p. 27)). Did Rashad owe any money?" The Imam looked over to his parents. They both nodded no. Alhamdulillaah their family was wealthy, so they never had to borrow from anyone masha'Allaah.

"Alhamdulillaah, in that case we can proceed to the next topic, and that is weeping and mourning over the dead. The Prophet (PBUH) allowed weeping quietly for the deceased, as long as it isn't wailing.

"He also said it is permissible for a woman to mourn for a maximum period of three days over the death of someone other than her husband. The Messenger of Allaah (PBUH) said:

"It is not permissible for a woman who believes in Allaah and the Last Day to mourn over a dead person more than three days, except for her husband, where she mourns for four months and ten days."
(Bukhari)

"A point to note is the reason for all the ahadith referring to women mourning is because mourning is not an attribute of men." (Shaykh al-Jibaly)

"Now let's move onto the procedure for washing the deceased person. Usually the person who died will be washed by the Muslims of the same gender, males will be washed by males and females will be washed by females, insha'Allaah (Ahmad and Abu Dawud). Washing a dead body is a great act, and all Muslims should be encouraged to do it. The Prophet (PBUH) said:

"He who washes a Muslim and conceals what he sees (i.e. bad odors, appearance, and anything loathsome), Allaah grants him forgiveness forty times (or for forty major sins)..."(Al-Hakim, al-Bayhaqi)

"In order to be eligible for this reward, a Muslim should only seek Allaah's Pleasure, and not worldly reward. After washing the dead body one must wash their hands well. Some people prefer to take a bath, but according to many scholars and ahadith, this is not necessary, although it is recommended (ad-Daaraqutni and al-Khatib in at-Tarikh. Verified to be authentic by al-Hafiz Ibn Hajar and al-Albani (Ahkaam ul-Janaa'iz 72)).

"There is a procedure to follow when washing the deceased, and insha'Allaah some of you will be able to experience that in time. After the body is washed you will need to shroud the body; you will need 3 pieces of cloth to wrap the body in as this was the number the Prophet (PBUH) was shrouded in (Abu Dawud, an-Nasa'l). Although it will be less than 3 when a man dies in ihraam as he will then be buried in the same 2 pieces of cloth, as I mentioned earlier..

"The Messenger of Allaah (PBUH) said:

"Wear white clothes, for verily it is among the best of your garments, and shroud your dead in it also."
(Abu Dawud, at-Tirmithi)

"Insha'Allaah, you will see all the procedures of washing and shrouding when you experience washing a dead body hands-on. After the body is wrapped up in the cloth, then the janaazah is carried to the place of prayer for the funeral prayer to take place, known in Arabic as salaat-ul janaazah. Praying salaat-ul janaazah is a communal obligation - fard kifaayah; if someone is buried without it being performed, the whole community incurs a sin for not having fulfilled this obligation.

"I want all of the brothers to try and attend the prayer for the deceased even if you do not know him/her. Remember that the entire janaazah prayer is said standing only, there are no rukoo ' or sujoods. Does anyone know why?

"I know," Wali replied. "It's because the body is placed in front of the Imam during the janaazah prayer, and if we did rukoo ' or sujood it would appear to the layman that we are worshiping the body, authubillaah."

"That's absolutely right, Wali, masha'Allaah," the Imam said, and he continued with the rest of the halaqah. "Like any other prayer, this prayer is also performed facing the Qiblah. Okay, I want to tell you how the janaazah will be performed, especially for the sisters who will not be attending tomorrow, insha'Allaah. Some information you might want to know before the prayer takes place insha'Allaah:

1. The washed and shrouded body is brought to the musallaa, and placed at the front, towards the Qiblah.
2. The Imam stands at the front, and there should be an odd number of rows behind him. The body of the deceased should be kept in front of the Imam.
3. The Imam should face the Qiblah and stand near the head of the body if the deceased is a male, and by the mid-section if the deceased is a female.
4. If the prayer is to be offered for more than one person, then the bodies should be placed one in front of the other; the male body being closest to the Imam and the female body further away.

"That is basically it. There are more details, but the brothers will see that first hand and experience it tomorrow with Rashad's body insha'Allaah. Does anyone have any questions about the procedure?" Everyone was looking around at this time and no one said anything.

"Tomorrow is a big day, I think it is almost Isha time, why don't we all make ablution and get ready for prayer?" Grandpa said. Everyone knew he was right, and got up and headed for the restrooms. As Zeba was going to the restroom upstairs, she looked around and noticed how empty the house was without Rashad.

"What a big house, every luxury in the world in it, but it means nothing when there is no one to share it with. In the end none of these things matter, yet people strive for all this, day and night. In the end it is only our deeds that matter." Zeba was just talking to herself.

"Zeba, you seem to be a thousand miles away, what are you thinking about?" asked Sarah.

"You are so wise for your age, Sarah. I was just thinking about what a big house this is, and how Rashad had everything he ever wanted, yet he isn't taking any of it with him. It's so sad to wake up and know at the end of the day, it is only our deeds that count, yet millions of people strive for their desires and materialistic stuff," Zeba replied.

"You know I bet Rashad wishes he could have done more prayers now, helped more people, read more Qur'aan, fasted more. Yaa Allaah! What he would have given up for all of those deeds now!" Sarah sighed.

"Your right, Sarah, except it's too late now. This is why we have to always be living as if we will die at any given moment. We can't rely on tomorrow to repent and do good deeds. We need to make today count!" Zeba said. Mom was slowly coming up the stairs, and overheard the two girls talking.

"Well said, Zeba! You're absolutely correct; we cannot depend on tomorrow to save us, for no one is promised tomorrow. No one is promised the next second in life. Therefore, we must all act as if this is it for us, and if this is it, are we ready to meet Allaah (SWT)? You know if our actions and words are in sync, that really helps us to get to another level. So often people say things, but they never act on it, and so often they do things, but their speech is the opposite of their actions," Mom said. Both Zeba and Sarah nodded their heads and knew that Mom was right.

"Who's next for the restroom?" Fatima asked, as she was dripping with water from her wudhu. Zeba and Sarah looked at Mom since she was the eldest, they gestured for her to go ahead.

"Jazaakuma-Allaahu khayran, girls," Mom said, as she headed for the restroom.

"Tonight feels like the longest night of my life," Fatima sighed, as she passed Zeba and Sarah to get ready for prayer. Zeba looked at Sarah and they both felt what Fatima just said.

"May Allaah (SWT) give us all patience to get through this ordeal, Ameen," was Zeba's response.

"Ameen," said Sarah.

Isha prayer was over and everyone was now getting ready for bed.

Grandma lied next to Zeba. "Zeba, what do you think of all of this? Is it scary to know that this could happen to any of us? Many people think that their lives are great and that they have enough time to do as they wish in their life. Then they will shape up and repent later, and live life according to the Islamic way," said Grandma.

"Astaghfirullaah, life doesn't go as we plan it; it goes as Allaah (SWT) plans it. We all need to be ready for death at any moment. Therefore Grandma, we always need to be doing what is right, and keep ourselves on the right track, insha'Allaah, because it could be our last breath at any moment," Zeba replied, while tears were burning her eyes.

"Zeba, let's say our du'aas, and get some rest honey, we have a long day ahead of us, insha'Allaah," Grandma advised.

"Okay, Grandma," said Zeba. Both of them silently said their du'aas, and then closed their eyes and fell asleep.

"I am so exhausted, but I can't sleep," Uncle Zakariya said to Aunt Khadija, as they lay in bed.

"I know me too. All I keep thinking about is Rashad, and what he must be facing right now. I never imagined this day . . . would be here so soon." Aunt Khadija said. "Do you remember when Rashad was born? What a beautiful baby he was, masha' Allaah. Do you remember when he first started to crawl?" said aunt Khadija. As she said this, Aunt Khadija and Uncle Zakariya cried silently, each in their own thoughts about Rashad.

"Allaah burdens not a person beyond his scope"
(Quran Chapter 2: Verse 286)

Accepting your fate; what does that mean? Most people, when they find out that they will die, they will be in denial. Maybe that's why Allaah (SWT) takes our life in different ways. For then no one is prepared. Alhamdulillaah, He (SWT) knows that the majority of people in the world do not want to die, but live for their desires. They want to enjoy this world as much as they can; get married, have kids, watch the kids grow up and get married, have grandkids, make money, go on vacations, etc. So death is not really accepted. Death is looked upon as an evil thing that has to happen to people.

Often we hear people say, 'Why? Why did so and so die? He was so young, or she didn't do anything to anyone'. There is always constant regret. They are hurt and in pain. Many people get depressed over deaths, and never get back to normality. It is becoming more and more difficult for people to leave this world behind. They think of death as something one faces at old age; when they have done everything their hearts desire. Even then most people don't want to die. They do everything in their power to stay young and alive; eat healthy, exercise, take pills, and even cosmetic surgery. Many people react this way because they have no idea why they are living. They are unaware as to what the purpose of life is. They have no idea why we were created, or who created us. However, people who have faith in Allaah (SWT), God the Exalted; their view of life is somewhat different. Allaah (SWT) tells us the purpose of our existence in the Qur'aan:

"And I did not create the jinn and mankind except to worship Me." **(The Qur'aan 51:56)**

"The One who created death and life, that He may test you as to which of you is best in deed. And He is the Almighty, the Forgiving." **(The Qur'aan 67:2)**

We know that we were brought to this life to be tested; to see if we can control our desires and follow the straight path. Unfortunately, this is not the case for everyone. A large percentage of the world's population is unaware of the teachings of their religions, and therefore is unable to practice it correctly. This is partly due to what Satan is feeding them, and partly due to a result of what they want to feed themselves. They don't want to learn the truth, they don't want to follow the right path, and they don't want to leave their desires.

We have a population of about 6 billion people on earth, and the majority of them have no purpose or idea of why we were even created. I have seen so many people suffering from illnesses, sadness, depression, and many other problems due to their lack of faith; when one has nothing to look forward to, then why should he/she do his/her best in this life? Why not give up? Why not be upset and angry all of the time? Why not steal, commit burglary, commit adultery, fornication, drugs, drinking, etc? *"This is it. You only live once. Live it the best way you can."* I hear these words all the time, yet it is these people who are never satisfied with what they have. They always want more. I am not saying to not want more in life. I am just saying that we should understand why we are here, and then strive for this life as well as the hereafter, making the hereafter our primary goal. When we can align our minds, body and soul in one direction we will have peace and contentment. This is difficult to achieve unless one truly digs deep within themselves, and endeavors to seek knowledge and discover who they are. One suggestion to help achieve this is reading the Books of Allaah (SWT), God the Exalted. Who better to tell us why we exist than the One Who created us. I would suggest reading the Qur'aan, for those are the words of God Almighty Himself. Wouldn't it be amazing to see what God Almighty has told us? Contemplate on that Book as well as on the original Gospel sent to Jesus (PBUH), and the original Torah, if you can find any of the latter two.

The Qur'aan is the only book of Allaah (SWT), God the Exalted, where a word has not changed in over 1400 years:

"Indeed, it is We who sent down the message [i.e. the Qur'aan], and indeed We will be its guardian." **(The Qur'aan 15:9)**

Isn't that in itself a good enough reason to read this book, and see what it has to say? Let alone the fact that millions have memorized this book in their hearts and minds over these past 1400 years and still continue to do so, and that it is recited daily by over 1 billion Muslims all over the world. Knowledge truly is power! Everyone should try to obtain knowledge and gain an understanding of what life is really about, and discover the true meaning of our existence. Of course there will always be people who don't agree, but it's worth reading and contemplating. What do you have to lose?

Now that you have discovered the purpose of life, the next stage is to find out how to live your life according to this new knowledge that you have acquired. How will you live your life if you knew the purpose and reason for your existence? Will you still behave the same way after you have acquired knowledge that probably doesn't approve much of your lifestyle? Or will you change? Will you act and behave in accordance with what your purpose in life is? All of these questions and more enable an individual to realize if they are aligned with their thoughts, words, actions, habits and character. Understanding what will happen when one dies is what I want to cover next. Different people have different views. As for the monotheistic religions in the world; Islam, Christianity and Judaism, they believe in a Day of Resurrection. That means, that once you're dead, life is not over, there is a day that all humans will be resurrected and they have to answer for what they have done while they were living:

"Every soul shall taste death. And only on the Day of Resurrection will you be given your full compensation. Whoever is removed from the Fire and admitted to Jannah (Heaven) has surely attained success. And what is the life of this world except the enjoyment of delusion."
(The Qur'aan 3:185)

Once you have a clear understanding of where you are heading afterwards, then you have a picture in your mind of what your final destination looks like. Your understanding of what happens in the hereafter will ease your mind, and put everything in perspective. Are you living according to the way you ought to? Once you are able to solve these issues and more, we can discuss death. No one can escape death, even if they tried:

"Wherever you may be, death will overtake you, even if you were in fortresses built up strong and high."
(The Qur'aan 4:78)

Over the years many people have tried many different techniques to stay young forever. None of those methods have worked. All that they have done is 'masked' the signs of ageing. It's vital to understand that death is inevitable; that every living thing in this planet will die. Nothing and no one will live forever:

"Say: Verily the death from which you flee will meet you; then you will be returned to the Knower of the unseen and the witnessed, and He will inform you about what you used to do."(The Qur'aan 62:8)

Knowing this fact will help you understand that life and death are a part of every living being's destiny. Again, having peace in death and dying, comes from living. Living in the way we are supposed to live; living life with a purpose and reason; living life knowing why we were created, and what our final destination is. Often people give up on life; many commit suicide, kill others, and commit other horrific acts. People behave this way because they don't know any better; because they don't have enough meaning in their lives to change; because there is no purpose in their lives. Many people also assume that their actions will not in return affect them. Those who believe in Allaah (SWT), Glory be to Him, know that every sane adult will be accountable for his/her deeds. They know that they are to be patient in times of conflict and happiness; that tests and trials are there to test one's patience and gratitude, and are also a means of attaining Allaah's Forgiveness:

"The Prophet (PBUH) said, "Whatever befalls the believer: thirst, fatigue, worry, sadness, depression, harm, even if a thorn pierces his body, but a forgiveness from Allaah follows that.(Bukhari & Muslim)

We need to remember Allaah (SWT) at all times, in all seasons, and in pain as well as joy. We need to remember that after a long rain storm there is sunshine, and that this life is a test, and we will return to our Lord. This life is just a test and only those who are true to themselves will pass this test. Those who wish to change and be righteous will be given what they deserve. We need the desire and motivation to want to change and seek the truth. The truth exists; whether we want to see it or not is up to us. We need to use our minds and contemplate on the truth. The below is an excerpt from Shaykh 'Aid al-Qarni's book 'Don't Be Sad'. I feel it is appropriate to mention here, as it shows how fortunate we are *masha'Allaah*:

Read it and don't be sad!

If you are stricken by poverty, others are chained in debt.
If you don't have shoes, others have no feet.
If you feel pain now, others have been aching for years.
If your son dies, others have lost many.

If you have sinned, then repent.
If you have committed a mistake, correct it.
The doors of repentance are ever open!
The fountain of forgiveness is ever rich!
So, don't be sad!

Let all bygones be bygones!
What is predestined for you, you shall see it!
Being sad will not change anything!
So don't be sad!

Sadness spoils your life!
Destroys your happiness!
And turns it into wretchedness!
So don't be sad!

Supplication is your shield!
Prayer is your beacon!
Prostration is your means!
So don't be sad!

See how vast is the earth!
How nice are the gardens and forests!
How bright are the stars!
All are happy, but you are sad!
So, don't be sad!

You have sweet water to drink!
Fresh air to breathe!
Feet to walk with!
You sleep safely in your bed!
So, why be sad?

Every cloud has a silver lining!
After long nights, come the bright suns!
Life will soon give you a smile!
So be ready to get it!
And don't be sad!

Real life is that spent in happiness!
So cross out your sad days from your age!
Peace of mind is the real treasure!
Sorrow avails not!
So don't be sad!

Chapter

2

The Power
Of
Prayer

"Wali, wake up. It's almost Fajr prayer," said Grandpa.

"Okay, Grandpa I'm up. 'Al-Hamdu lillaahi-ladhee 'ahyaanaa ba'da maa 'amaatanaa wa'ilayhin-nushoor (Praise be to Allaah Who gives us life after He has caused us to die, and to Him is the return)," Wali said, as he got out of bed. It always felt great to be able to say the morning du'aa. Wali pondered for a moment how Rashad would not be able to say the du'aas anymore. What a blessing it is to be able to still have the ability to make du'aa he thought. Everyone was rushing to the bathrooms, except Uncle Zakariya's family. They weren't used to waking up for Fajr prayer.

"I know that Zakariya isn't used to waking up for Fajr, but he should today, and beg Allaah for His Mercy upon his son," Grandpa said to Mother.

Mom agreed, "I will go and wake him up insha'Allaah," she said. "Zakariya, wake up. It is prayer time."

"I'm up. Khadija, please wake up . . . it is prayer time. We all need to pray, will you please wake the girls up as well," Uncle Zakariya whispered softly.

"Bismil-laahir-Rahmaanir-Raheem. Yes, I will wake them up," Aunt Khadija replied.

"Zeba, hurry up, there is a line for the bathroom," Mom said. Zeba was just finishing up her wudhu (ablution), and had thought she was the last to go to the bathroom, so she was taking her sweet old time. She didn't know her cousins were up and also needed to wash up. It had been a long time since Fatima and Sarah had arisen for Fajr prayer. They were so tired, but they wanted to pray too. They both jumped out of bed, as their mom called for them.

It was then that the adhaan (call to prayer) went off in the kitchen (Wali had brought his portable clock with him and set it in the kitchen):

"Allāhu Akbar Allāhu Akbar,   Allāhu Akbar   Allāhu Akbar.
(Allah is Great (said four times)

Ash-hadu an-lā ilāha illallāh, Ash-hadu an-lā ilāha illallāh, (I bear witness that there is no god except the One God (Allah). (said two times))

Ash-hadu anna Muḥammadan rasūlullāh, Ash-hadu anna Muḥammadan rasūlullāh, (I bear witness that Muhammad is the messenger of Allah. (said two times))

Hayya 'alas-salāh, Hayya 'alas-salāh,(Hurry to prayer (Rise up for prayer) (said two times))

Hayya 'alal-falāḥ, Hayya 'alal-falāḥ, (Hurry to success (Rise up for Salvation) (said two times))

As-salaatu khayrun minan-nawm, As-salaatu khayrun minan-nawm, (Prayer is better than sleep (said two times))

Allāhu Akbar- Allāhu Akbar, (Allah is Great) (said two times))

Lā ilāha illallāh." (There is no god except the One God (Allah))

Everyone sat silently and said the du'aa after the adhaan finished. They all stood up and prayed Fajr. "SubhaanAllaah! What a morning that we are all standing and praying Fajr together. I just wish it wasn't under these circumstances. I wish that Rashad could also be standing with us and praying," Grandma thought, as she looked at everyone. It was then that everyone heard someone crying . . . it was Aunt Khadija; she was prostrating on the prayer rug, and crying. She was begging Allaah to have mercy on her son.

Mom was sitting right next to her and just finished supplicating when she heard Aunt Khadija saying, "I know that Rashad didn't pray much. I know that he was only thinking about enjoying himself all the time, and how to get ahead in this world. This is my fault. This is all that his father and I taught him. We didn't think he would die so soon. Yaa Allaah! I also know that You are the Most

Forgiving and Most Merciful; please forgive Rashad for his sins. Please let him enter paradise through Your Mercy. I promise you that insha'Allaah I will change myself, and how my family is; we will all pray on time insha'Allaah, we will learn more about Islam, and we will follow the rules that You have set for us." Even though Aunt Khadija was not loud, those closest to her could hear her mumbling and crying. Everyone had tears in their eyes . . . and supplicated to Allaah (SWT) to forgive Rashad for his sins. They begged for forgiveness for themselves and all the Muslims in the world.

"I love praying in congregation. There is something so inspiring about it to me," Zeba whispered to Sarah. Sarah nodded while in her own thoughts; thinking about how peaceful it really was this morning, praying. Zeba felt so calm and the power of reciting the verses from the Qur'aan made tears flow from her eyes. For the first time, she was actually thinking of the meaning of each verse as she recited it.

Grandpa turned around and said, "I wonder if Rashad thought about his last prayer; that it was going to be his last. I want you guys to remember these words every time you pray; 'This could be my last prayer'." Everyone just pondered over the words, and rose up from the floor and started to put the prayer rugs away.

Are you ready to turn to your Lord; Lord of the universe, and repent? This is a touchy subject for millions, if not billions of people. They have no idea as to why they should repent. Many people feel they have done nothing wrong to repent from. Others feel they don't need to repent. Some have no idea who they should repent to, and fail to acknowledge the Creator, thus feeling that all they have achieved is due to their own efforts. If there is no Creator, then why should one repent? Allaah (SWT), God the Exalted, is not given credit for all that He has done for mankind. Yet, Allaah (SWT) is Most Forbearing, and keeps giving to His creation, without asking for anything in return. How sad is it that we don't recognize that; that we think we don't owe anything to Allaah (SWT).

For Muslims, prayer is a must; five times a day. Personally, I am glad that it is five times a day, for I love being close to my Creator. During prayer is when I feel the closest to Him. The purpose of *salaah* (prayer) is primarily to act as an individual's communion with God; Allaah (SWT). It enables one to stand in front of God, thank and praise Him, and ask Him to show us the "right path" (as mentioned in *Surah al-Faatihah* (the first *surah* in the Qur'aan) which is recited in every prayer). In addition, the daily prayers serve as a constant reminder to Muslims that they should be grateful for God's blessings. It ensures that every Muslim prioritizes Islam over all other concerns, thereby revolving their life around God, and submitting to His Will. Prayer also serves as a formal method of remembering God. In the Qur'aan it is mentioned that:

*"The true believers are those who feel a fear in their hearts (of the consequences of violating the commands of Allaah) when Allaah is mentioned. And when His verses are recited to them, they find their faith strengthened. They put their trust in their Lord."(The **Qur'aan 8:2**)*

Allaah (SWT) also states in The Qur'aan:

"Those whose hearts when Allaah is mentioned, are filled with fear, who show patient perseverance over their afflictions, keep up regular prayer, and spend (in charity) out of what We have bestowed upon them."
(The Qur'aan 22:35)

The *salaah* (prayer) is also mentioned as a means to restrain the believer from social wrong and moral deviancy **(The Qur'aan 29:45)**.

It is during acts of worship such as praying *salaah* (prayer), reciting the Qur'aan, dhikr (remembrance of Allaah (SWT)), that one draws closer to Allaah (SWT). It is at this time that one often reflects on his/her actions; the good and the bad deeds. This is the time to repent and ask for forgiveness, as no one is perfect, and we all make mistakes. We should learn from our mistakes, ask for forgiveness from Allaah, God the Greatest, and strive to not repeat them. One should want to better oneself and want to change. Only through change are we able to grow.

This day that might be the last day of your life, are you sitting on a prayer rug, and praying? Are you crying as you're praying? Are you sad that you haven't been this sincere for a long time? Are you wondering if you will be forgiven or not? Are you scared of what you're going to face soon? The problem with praying and repenting in the last minute could mean many things.

Firstly, one can never be sure when one's last minute will be, so delaying these actions could be the worst decision a person makes in his/her life. It might be too late! It could mean that you feel you might be forgiven for all that you have done, because you waited so long. It could also mean that your prayers were not sufficient for Allaah (SWT) and they won't be accepted.

Next, you may wish that you had prayed a lot more; that you felt you were closer to your Lord; that you had done as He has asked you to do. You may wish that Allaah (SWT) takes care of your children, spouse, parents, family and friends in your absence. On this day will you cry as you pray? Will you ask for everything you have always wanted? On this day will you remember no one but yourself? Will you just want some kind of affirmation that you will be okay in the next life? Amazing, we all want this in one way or another, but many are not doing anything about it.

If today was your LAST day, you would be acting so different in terms of your prayers and your connection with Allaah (SWT). You wouldn't think twice about the many things you normally think about. You would control your thoughts, words, actions, habits, and character, this day. This day everything will be as you have wanted it to have been all of your life. You are doing everything you can to perfect this day, and you are satisfied. **The BIG question is, then why isn't everyday spent like this?** Why are we prolonging this feeling of being complete and sane for the last day that we are alive? If prayer can do this to us, then why aren't we praying? If most of us want to be that close to the Lord of the universe, then why aren't we? Why is it something we are holding off until the last minute? Why don't we want to feel this way right now? What if we don't have that last day to do all of this? What if today is our LAST day? No one is promised the next moment, forget a whole day.

If today was your LAST day then wouldn't you want to die in a state of peace? These are all questions one should ponder. I know, because a few years ago I never pondered these thoughts. I too wanted to live a long life and enjoy this world. I don't know what I did to deserve it, but Allaah (SWT) enlightened me, and guided me to a path that I have had the most peace with. A path that none can take away from me except Allaah (SWT). No amount of money, gold, and silver will give me the peace that my Lord, Allaah (SWT), has given me, *alhamdulillaah* (All praise is for God). I have searched for the truth for years in many ways; in science, psychology, humans, and various religions. Only Islam has allowed me to fill the emptiness that no one else could fulfill. It is the most powerful feeling ever. Unfortunately many will never feel this ecstasy of faith, yet should they feel it, they won't want anything to replace it.

Think about your last day and what you want to be doing on this day; would this be the day that you will pick up the Book of Allaah (SWT) to reflect on His Words? Would you read the Qur'aan and ponder over the wisdom behind it? Would you actually cry at some of the passages as the truth becomes apparent to you? These are all questions one should ask oneself.

Some of us feel we have life figured out, and we plan and plot our lives as if we are going to live forever. Unfortunately that's not true. Our life is plotted and planted to a certain degree. There will be many things that we want in this life, and we strive for and for some reason or another we don't obtain it. It's usually because Allaah (SWT); God Almighty has other plans for us; He, Lord of the universe, knows better and doesn't see that certain thing as being good for us:

"....and it may be that you dislike a thing which is good for you and that you like a thing which is bad for you. Allâh knows but you do not know."
(The Qur'aan 2:216)

Many incidences and occurrences in one's life leave people wondering and questioning how it happened. Where it came from? It was never meant to be that way. Again in the scheme of plotting and planning, Allaah (SWT) is also planning. Wouldn't you like to understand all of this? If there truly is a God of the universe, is it not fair to find out who He is? Is it not fair to understand His Wisdom, and reasons for our existence on earth? All of these questions and more are all answered in the Qur'aan. Isn't it unfair to not read a book which hasn't had a single word changed for the last 1400 years? If this is truly the Word of God the Greatest, the Most Merciful, shouldn't we strive to get acquainted with those Words? It is only through those Words that one will truly find solace and peace. What if you read those Words and truly found out the purpose to life, would you be a different person for the rest of your life? Would your life be how you imagined it to be? Would you be at peace as you are finally treading on the path of those who have been amongst the most righteous? These are all questions one should ponder. The story below is a beautiful example, one that makes you really think:

***'Destination the Hereafter - Have you packed your suitcases?'* From Az-Zaman Al-Qaadim compiled by Abdul-Malik Al-Qasim. Translated by Muhammad Alshareef**

Her cheeks were worn and sunken and her skin hugged her bones. That didn't stop her though; you could never catch her not reciting *Qur'aan*. Always vigil in her personal prayer room Dad had set up for her. Bowing, prostrating and raising her hands in prayer. That was the way she was from dawn to sunset and back again, boredom was for others.

As for me I craved nothing more than fashion magazines and novels. I treated myself all the time to videos until those trips to the rental place became my trademark. As they say, when something becomes habit people tend to distinguish you by it. I was negligent in my responsibilities and laziness characterized my salaah.

One night, I turned the video off after a marathon three hours of watching. The adhaan softly rose in that quiet night. I slipped peacefully into my blanket.

Her voice carried from her prayer room. "Yes? Would you like anything? Noorah?"

With a sharp needle she popped my plans. "Don't sleep before you pray Fajr!"

"Agh . . . there's still an hour before Fajr that was only the first Adhaan!"

With those loving pinches of hers, she called me closer. She was always like that, even before the fierce sickness shook her spirit and shut her in bed.

"Hanan can you come sit beside me."

I could never refuse any of her requests; you could touch the purity and sincerity. "Yes? Noorah."

"Please sit here."

"OK, I'm sitting. What's on your mind?"

With the sweetest mono voice she began reciting:

Every soul shall taste death and you will merely be repaid your earnings on Resurrection Day.

She stopped thoughtfully. Then she asked, "Do you believe in death?"

"Of course I do."

"Do you believe that you shall be responsible for whatever you do, regardless of how small or large?"

"I do, but Allaah is Forgiving and Merciful and I've got a long life waiting for me."

"Stop it Hanan . . . aren't you afraid of death and its abruptness? Look at Hind. She was younger than you but she died in a car accident. So did so-and so, and so-and so. Death is age-blind and your age could never be a measure of when you shall die."

The darkness of the room filled my skin with fear. "I'm scared of the dark and now you made me scared of death, how am I supposed to go to sleep now? Noorah, I thought you promised you'd go with us on vacation during the summer break."

Her voice broke and her heart quivered. "I might be going on a long trip this year Hanan, but somewhere else. Just may be. All of our lives are in Allaah's Hands and we all belong to Him."

My eyes welled and the tears slipped down both cheeks.

I pondered my sisters grizzly sickness, how the doctors had informed my father privately that there was not much hope that Noorah was going to outlive the disease. She wasn't told though. Who hinted to her? Or was it that she could sense the truth?

"What are you thinking about Hanan?" Her voice was sharp. "Do you think I am just saying this because I am sick? Uh-uh. In fact, I may live longer than people who are not sick. And you Hanan, how long are you going to live? Twenty years, may be? Forty? Then what?" Through the dark she reached for my hand and squeezed gently. "There's no difference between us; we're all going to leave this world to live in Paradise or agonize in Hell. Listen to the words of Allaah: "Anyone who is pushed away from the Fire and shown into Jannah will have triumphed."

I left my sister's room dazed, her words ringing in my ears: May Allaah guide you Hanan - don't forget your prayer.

Eight o'clock in the morning, pounding on my door. I don't usually wake up at this time. Crying, Confusion, O Allaah, what happened?

Noorahs condition became critical after Fajr, they took her immediately to the Hospital . . . Innaa lillaahi wa innaa ilayhi raaji'oon.

There wasn't going to be any trips this summer. It was written that I would spend the summer at home.

After an eternity . . . it was one o'clock in the afternoon. Mother phoned the hospital. "Yes. You can come and see her now." Dad's voice had changed, Mother could sense something had gone deathly wrong. We left immediately.

Where was that avenue I used to travel and thought was so short? Why was it so long now, so very long? Where was the cherished crowd and traffic that would give me a chance to gaze left and right. Everyone just moved out of our way. Mother was shaking her head in her hands . . . crying . . . as she made du'aa for her Noorah.

We arrived at the hospitals main entrance.

One man was moaning another was involved in an accident and a third's eyes were iced; you couldn't tell if he was alive or dead.

We skipped stairs to Noorahs floor. She was in intensive care.

The nurse approached us. "Let me take you to her." As we walked down the aisles the nurse went on expressing how sweet a girl Noorah was. She reassured Mother somewhat that Noorah's condition had gotten better than what it was in the morning.

"Sorry. No more than one visitor at a time." This was the intensive care unit. Through the small window in the door and past the flurry of white robes I caught my sister's eyes. Mother was standing beside her. After two minutes, Mother came out unable to control her crying.

"You may enter and say Salaam to her on condition that you do not speak too long," they told me. Two minutes should be enough."

"How are you, Noorah? You were fine last night sister, what happened?"

We held hands, she squeezed harmlessly. "Even now, alhamdulillaah, I'm doing fine."

"Alhamdulillaah . . . but . . . your hands are so cold."

I sat on her bedside and rested my fingers on her knee. She jerked it away.

"Sorry . . . did I hurt you?"

"No, it is just that I remembered Allaah's Words: "One leg will be wrapped to the other leg (in the death shroud)."

" . . . Hanan pray for me. I may be meeting the first day of the hereafter very soon. It is a long journey and I haven't prepared enough good deeds in my suitcase.

A tear escaped my eye and ran down my cheek at her words. I cried and she joined me. The room blurred away and left us . . . two sisters - to cry together. Rivulets of tears splashed down on my sister's palm which I held with both hands. Dad was now becoming more worried about me. I've never cried like that before.

At home and upstairs in my room, I watched the sun pass away with a sorrowful day. Silence mingled in our corridors. A cousin came in my room, another. The visitors were many and all the voices from downstairs stirred together. Only one thing was clear at that point . . . Noorah had died!

I stopped distinguishing who came and who went. I couldn't remember what they said. O Allaah, where was I? What was going on? I couldn't even cry anymore.

Later that week they told me what had happened. Dad had taken my hand to say goodbye to my sister for the last time, I had kissed Noorah's head.

I remember only one thing though, seeing her spread on that bed, the bed that she was going to die on. I remembered the verse she recited: "One leg will be wrapped to the other leg (in the death shroud)," and I knew too well the truth of the next verse: "The drive on that day will be to your Lord (Allaah)!"

I tiptoed into her prayer room that night. Staring at the quiet dressers and silenced mirrors, I treasured who it was that had shared my mother's stomach with me. Noorah was my twin sister.

I remembered who I had swapped sorrows with. Who had comforted my rainy days? I remembered who had prayed for my guidance and who had spent so many tears for so many long nights telling me about death and accountability.

May Allaah save us all.

Tonight is Noorah's first night that she shall spend in her tomb. O Allaah, have mercy on her and illumine her grave. This was her Qur'aan, her prayer mat and . . . and this was the spring rose-colored dress that she told me she would hide until she got married, the dress she wanted to keep just for her . . . husband.

I remembered my sister and cried over all the days that I had lost. I prayed to Allaah to have mercy on me, accept me and forgive me. I prayed to Allaah to keep her firm in her grave as she always liked to mention in her supplications.

At that moment, I stopped. I asked myself: what if it was I who had died? Where would I be moving on to? Fear pressed me and the tears began all over again.

Allaahu Akbar, Allaahu Akbar . . .

The first adhaan rose softly from the masjid, how beautiful it sounded this time. I felt calm and relaxed as I repeated the Muaddhins call. I wrapped the shawl around my shoulders and stood to pray Fajr. I prayed as if it was my last prayer, a farewell prayer, just like Noorah had done yesterday. It had been her last Fajr.

Now and insha'Allaah for the rest of my life, if I awake in the mornings I do not count on being alive by evening, and in the evening I do not count on being alive by morning. We are all going on Noorah's journey; . . . what have we prepared for it?

Chapter

3

Asking
For
Forgiveness

"Grandpa's words were strong . . . we never know when it will be our last prayer. So we have to make every prayer count. We have to make every prayer our best prayer. Seize the moment. Never take it for granted, for it can be our last one," Wali said, to Zeba, Sarah and Fatima.

"Life is too short to not think about meeting our Lord, and we have to be ready at all times, insha'Allaah," Zeba added. They all cleaned up, and then the men began to head out to the janaazah. Aunt Khadija began crying and just looked at Uncle Zakariya.

"I know, today is the day, Rashad's biggest test of his life. Just make du'aa for him. A mother's du'aa is powerful. We need everyone's du'aas, please," Uncle Zakariya pleaded, as he turned one last time to look at everyone.

"Let's go, son, it's time to go to the janaazah," Grandpa said to Uncle Zakariya. The ride to the janaazah seemed to take forever, even though it was only a ten minute drive. "Alhamdulillaah we are here, go and announce that we are here, and for everyone to please meet outside the mosque and get ready for the janaazah," Grandpa said. Wali went inside and informed the Imam.

"Everyone please meet outside for the janaazah, and then we will all drive to the graveyard to bury the body," the Imam said. The Imam lined the men into 3 straight rows, as the Prophet (PBUH) had done. Everyone faced the Qiblah (direction towards the Ka'bah), and the Imam stood by Rashad's head and lead the prayer. He raised his hands and said the first takbeer, and everyone followed. He then placed the palm of his right hand over the back of his left hand, wrist and arm, and held both hands tightly and recited silently, and again everyone followed. He then made the second takbeer and raised his hands, after which he and everyone else recited the salaah upon the Prophet (PBUH) silently. Then he made takbeer a third time, again raising his hands. This time he made du'aa for all the Muslims, including Rashad (silently). The du'aa recited is a well-known du'aa from the Sunnah:

'Allaahum-maghfir lihayyinaa, wa mayyitinaa, wa shaahidinaa, wa ghaa'ibinaa, wa sagheerinaa wa

kabeerinaa, wa dhakarinaa wa 'unthaanaa. Allaahumma man 'ahyaytahu minnaa fa'ahyihi 'alal-'Islaami, wa man tawaffaytahu minnaa fatawaffahu 'alal-'eemaani, Allaahumma laa tahrimnaa 'ajrahu wa laa tudhillanaa ba'dahu.'

(O Allaah! Forgive our living and dead, our present and absent, our young and old, and our males and our females. O Allaah! Whoever You keep alive, keep him alive upon Islam, and whoever you take away, take him in a state of eemaan (faith). O Allaah! Do not deny us the reward of (being afflicted with) him, and do not misguide us after him).

Then again, the Imam made another final takbeer, raising his hands, after which he turned to his right and made tasleem in a low voice:

'Assalamu-alaykum wa rahmat-Ullaah' (Peace be on you, and Allaah's Mercy).

Everyone followed the Imam silently; the janaazah prayer was finished. Everyone got into their cars, and headed out to the graveyard. Wali had never been so speechless. He had tears rolling down his face as did all the men in the family. They knew this was a journey everyone would take, and that they had better be prepared to face their Lord. As they reached the graveyard, each man wanted to participate in the burial.

After the burial was completed, the Imam made a du'aa to Allaah, and everyone else made supplications as well. When they were done, the Imam looked at all the men who were standing and said, "Today I will talk about forgiveness and the importance of it, before it is too late. How many of you have someone who is upset with you for one reason or another? Most of the time we do something that we know will hurt someone, but at that given moment we don't think about the consequences. Am I correct?" Everyone nodded. "Well, what happens if you hurt someone with your words, manners, or actions and they don't forgive you . . . as a matter of fact, they pray against you, for the pain that you have caused them.

"Did you know that Allaah (SWT) listens to all of His servant's prayers and supplications? Every nation and tribe was made by Allaah (SWT), so if we harm anyone, and they supplicate against us, then Allaah (SWT) could answer that person's supplication. The Prophet (PBUH) said:

"Fear the du'aa of he who has been wronged, for verily it ascends to the heaven faster than sparks (of light)".(Narrated by al-Hakim from 'Ibn Umar, and authenticated in Sahih al-Jaami' 118)

"Let me give you an example, say that you always have your TV on loud, and your neighbor has asked you nicely to turn it down several times, but you don't care. Well this neighbor cannot go to sleep at the time he wants to because of the nuisance that you are causing him, so then he is cranky when he reaches work and he doesn't do as good of a job as he could due to lack of sleep. You might say, 'that's his problem, not mine.'

"Well this neighbor, due to lack of his great performance doesn't receive a bonus or a raise, which in turn will make him/her very upset . . . so he supplicates to Allaah (SWT)- Lord of the worlds against you, that you too should not succeed in your endeavors, or that you move out of this apartment complex, etc. If Allaah answers his supplication, then one of those things might occur to you, and you will not understand why and where it came from. How many of you knew that?"

A few of the elders raised their hands, but all the youth were dumbfounded, except for Wali, who had raised his hand. Wali was home schooled so he had a lot of knowledge about Islam for a kid his age; he constantly read books, and went to any weekend classes that were offered at the masjid. He knew the power of knowledge, and also the need to use it.

"Look around, and see how many of you didn't know this. Now that you know, do you think you will be more careful in what you do? Do any of you want to hurt someone purposely and have them make supplication against you? Is it worth it? All of you have heard this saying- 'What goes around, comes around, right?' Be careful of all that you say and do. Allaah is always watching, and it is all getting recorded by the angels.

"You could get your punishment in this world as well as the hereafter . . . it's not worth it. Be God-conscience of all that you do. So, you're probably wondering by now what all of this has to do with forgiveness; what I want each and everyone of you to do today is to go to at least one person that you have harmed in any way, and ask that person for forgiveness. Ask for forgiveness and win their heart, before it is too late. You could do this by your words, by not doing what they dislike- giving up that habit, or by your actions; doing something great for them.

"I want to tell you about a hadith, about a time in the life of Prophet Muhammad (SAAW): A long time ago, in a land far, far away, there lived an old woman who was carrying a heavy load along the road in the desert. It was a bit difficult for her, but she was managing as best as she could. A man asked if he could help her with her load, and she readily obliged. Here is the conversation that transpired:

"It would be such a pleasure to have you come along with me. I accept your gracious offer of kindness and company," she said. She was a very talkative woman, and the young man did not want to interrupt her. So, he let her speak the entire time they were together without interruption:

"But as we walk along young man and as you help me with my load, I have only one request as we travel down this road: Don't talk to me about Muhammad! Because of him there is no peace and I have trouble in my mind. So, don't talk to me about Muhammad! And as we walk along together, we will get along just fine."
She continued:
"That man upsets me so, so much more than you could know! I hear of his name and reputation everywhere I go. Though his family and his clan once knew him as an honest man, he's dividing everyone with his claim that God is One!"

"He's misled all the weak, the poor, and the slaves. They think they've all found wealth and freedom by following his way!" she sarcastically snorted.

"He has corrupted all of our youth with his twisted brand of truth. He has convinced them that they all are strong and gave them somewhere to belong. So, don't you dare talk to me about Muhammad!"

They reached their destination, and the man helped the woman put away her belongings. The old woman, with a wide smile of gratitude for this stranger's kindness, turned to him, and said, "Thank you. Now, young man, you've really been so kind. That generosity and smile is very rare to find nowadays. Let me give you some advice, since you've been so very nice to me. Stay away from Muhammad. Don't heed his word or emulate his way. If you do, you will never have true peace, and all you will find is trouble."

As the young man turned to walk away, she stopped him: "Now before we part and go, if it's alright just the same, may I ask my dear young man, who are you? What's your name?"

He told her, and she stopped dead in her tracks.

"Forgive me, but what was that? Your words weren't very clear. My ears are getting old, and sometimes I have a hard time hearing. You know, it's truly rather funny, but I'm sure I must be wrong. Yet, I thought I heard you say that your name is Muhammad."

"I am Muhammad," the Prophet (peace be upon him) told the old woman.

She replied, "I bear witness there is nothing worthy of worship except God, and Muhammad is the Messenger of God."

"Oh, talk to me, Muhammad. Upon you I pray for peace for you have eased my troubled mind. Oh, talk to me, Muhammad and as we walk along together, we will get along just fine. As I travel down life's road I will get along just fine.'"

"This hadith shows us that just by the actions of Prophet Muhammad (SAAW); he was able to cause a woman who hated him to love him. He didn't say anything to her, just listened to her, and was patient as he helped her achieve where she wanted to go. It is our actions that speak louder than words. I often hear people fighting and arguing about topics they don't even have knowledge about. I always say, show me by your actions who you are, not just by your words.

"What is forgiveness according to Islam?" The Imam elaborated on the concept of forgiveness, and he began, "To receive forgiveness from Allaah there are three things one must do: firstly one must recognize the offense itself and its admission before Allaah. Secondly, one should make a commitment to never repeat the offense. Thirdly, one should ask Allaah for forgiveness. However if the offense was committed against another human being, or against society, a fourth condition is added: then they need to do whatever needs to be done to rectify the offense (within reason) and asking pardon of the offended party. Can everyone remember that formula for forgiveness?" Everyone nodded.

The Imam continued, "To end today's sermon, I want to leave all of you with this beautiful hadith qudsi #34: On the authority of Anas, who said: I heard Prophet Muhammad (PBUH) say:

"Allaah the Almighty has said: "O son of Adam, so long as you call upon Me and ask of Me, I shall forgive you for what you have done, and I shall not mind. O son of Adam, were your sins to reach the clouds of the sky and were you then to ask forgiveness of Me, I would forgive you. O son of Adam, were you to come to Me with sins nearly as great as the earth and were you then to face Me, ascribing no partner to Me, I would bring you forgiveness nearly as great as its."

By this time everyone had tears in their eyes. They knew how Forgiving Allaah (SWT) is, but this hadith deepened their love for their Lord. On that note, the Imam made one last du'aa, and they all departed their own ways. Uncle Zakariya was still standing at the grave of Rashad, with tears rolling down his face. He never thought the day *would come when he would bury his son. He always imagined his son burying him. How far was his thinking from the truth? Reality is different from what we imagine. This was his wake up call; life is too short to take for granted, not to do all the good deeds, for tomorrow is promised to no one. "Come on, Uncle Zakariya, let's get going," Wali said, as he put his arm around his uncle's shoulder. Wali was like a son to Uncle Zakariya, and now more than ever Uncle Zakariya needed him. They both headed out slowly to the car.*

Would you ask everyone you know for forgiveness? Forgiveness is something we all seek and need. It's an innate characteristic we possess, no matter who we are. Every human being at some point in their life needs forgiveness or wants to forgive others. Forgiveness lightens our hearts, and makes us feel everything will be alright. Forgiveness teaches us that we are not perfect. Forgiveness makes us realize that life is not perfect, and that we all need to remember that. Forgiveness helps put closure on the past, and brightens our future. Forgiveness humbles us. Forgiveness brings peace into our hearts, as well as others. Forgiveness makes us forget pride, and helps us judge situations based on the moment.

It takes a big person to forgive, and an even bigger person to ask for forgiveness. It takes a big person to love and look past the errors of others, and the mishaps they have suffered at the hands of others. It takes a big person to stop feeling the pain from the past and move onto the future. It takes a big person to change hate into love. By knowing this information, my question to you is, are you a BIG person? Many people find it difficult to forgive and forget. They hold on to bad thoughts and bad actions forever. They don't want to let go. For them it is easier to be upset all the time than to forgive. It's easier for some people to be spiteful than to let go. People have way too much pride; they don't want to be any less of a person than the next, so they don't forgive or ask for forgiveness. Pride, arrogance and conceitedness are all qualities which will cause nothing but harm in the long run. It's of no use; those feelings are all from Satan (Iblis):

"Iblis, the enemy of Allaah, envied Adam because Allaah honored Adam. He said, 'I was created from fire, and he was created from clay.' Therefore the first error ever committed was arrogance, for the enemy of Allaah was too arrogant to prostrate before Adam."
[Ibn Abi Hatim 1:123]

That is his works on you; he was expelled from the presence and Mercy of Allaah as a result of this arrogance, and he wants the same for us, authubillaah!

"No person who has the weight of a mustard seed of arrogance in his heart shall enter Paradise."
[Muslim 1:93]

Forgiveness, humility, humbleness are all qualities given by Allaah (SWT); these are the qualities one should aim for, and try to achieve. At the end of the day remember that you're the one holding on to the burden when you don't forgive. You're the one carrying the weight everywhere you go. You're the one really hurting. You think you are punishing the other person, but truly you are punishing yourself. You're giving yourself stress and ulcers from not forgiving and holding on to bad memories. I came across the following and thought I'd share it with you. It illustrates well how one's attitude affects one's life:

The Echo of Life

A man and his son were walking in the forest. Suddenly the boy trips and feeling a sharp pain, he screams, "AHHHH."
Surprised, he hears a voice coming from the mountain, "AHHHH!"
Filled with curiosity, he screams: "Who are you?", but the only answer he receives is: "Who are you?"
This makes him angry, so he screams: "You are a coward!" and the voice answers: "You are a coward!"
He looks at his father, asking, "Dad what is going on?"
"Son", the man replies, "Pay attention!" Then he screams, "I admire you!" The voice answers: "I admire you!"
The father shouts, "You are wonderful!", and the voice answers, "You are wonderful!"
The boy is surprised, but still can't understand what is going on. The father explains, "People call this an 'ECHO', but truly it is 'LIFE!' Life always gives you back what you give out! Life is a mirror of your actions. If you want more love, give more love. If you want more kindness, give more kindness. If you want understanding and respect, give understanding and respect. If you want people to be patient and respectful to you, give patience and respect!
This rule of Allaah (SWT) applies to every aspect of our lives."

Life always gives you back what you give out.
Your life is not coincidence; but a mirror of your own doings.

(Unknown Author)

Guilt

Guilt is a feeling humans feel when they know they did something wrong and they have to change that situation, but they don't. Guilt takes away your power and makes you a victim. It's not wrong to feel guilty; however one should not let guilt ruin their lives as all guilt is going to do is misdirect energy and make you feel weak. No one is perfect, and I feel guilty for many things that I have done in the past. However, I have also repented and begged for forgiveness from Allaah (SWT), and asked forgiveness for those I have hurt in the past. I also know that Allaah (SWT) is Most Forgiving, so beyond that I can't do anymore.

The past doesn't exist anymore, so why should guilt exist? Guilt should exist if it means it makes you beg for forgiveness from your Creator, and those you have hurt, and makes you a better person. Only then will one truly feel what repentance is, which will then cause one to feel peace and tranquility. Guilt is great as long as one can learn from it and repent from it. Once that stage is over, guilt can be put in the back of the closet. It's time to go to the next step.

Forgiving Yourself

How can you forgive yourself? Forgiving oneself is just like any other process, and it takes some time. You have to start by making a decision to forgive yourself; you do that by taking steps to change yourself. If this was the last day you were alive, you would need to forgive yourself and everyone else. There would be no turning back. There would only be one chance to make the right choice, and make it fast. There would only be one moment to take action on it, and that would be NOW! For what time you have left, make a difference and change; forgive not only yourself, but everyone who has hurt you. If you have already tried then seek forgiveness one last time. If people choose not to forgive you then that's their bad. The Prophet (PBUH) said that:

"Whoever apologizes to his brother and that apology is not accepted, then the person who refuses to accept the apology bears the sin of one who takes the property of another unjustly."

Sometimes it takes time for people to forgive as maybe the wounds are still fresh. Maybe they need more time to understand, and they themselves have been hurt too often. You have to let people be, and just do your part. After you go through this process you will feel much better, and lighter. If anything it will prove to everyone that you had the guts to ask for forgiveness, and are serious about wanting to change yourself, even if it was your last day alive on this earth. At least you're doing your part, and that's what counts.

Imagine today is NOT your last day, yet you did all of this. How will your heart feel? No one knows when death will approach them. Don't you want to be ready for that moment? Forgiveness is a blessing to have in this world; to die in peace. Isn't that something we should seek to achieve? I am asking you, let's do this now. Don't wait until tomorrow to begin. Begin this journey immediately and change for the better, as this could be your last day to live.

Genuine forgiveness takes time; unfortunately, sometimes it takes more time than we have. But we need to start somewhere. We need to start now! Remember that a person who cannot forgive, cannot dream; simply because that person is always busy looking at their past, and doesn't have time to look into the future. Take yourself for example, if you're constantly looking behind you as you're walking, can you see where you're headed?

Know this, that when you cannot forgive yourself or someone else, you are actually abusing yourself to some degree. How can you have contentment if you are abusing yourself? Contentment comes from peace and tranquility. I hope that now you are starting to see the value of forgiveness. Forgiveness is powerful, only if we use it. We need to learn how to forgive, and also be able to ask for forgiveness of others.

A great story I want to share with you; there was a man and he was walking with his wife, when all of a sudden he experienced a heart attack. At that same moment a pastor of a church was walking by, and the wife yelled for help. He went to the man, to help him, while his wife ran inside to call 911. The man who was dying, started asking the pastor for forgiveness, except he was saying his son's name, James. He kept saying, *"James forgive me, James forgive me"*. He was so out of breath and moments later he died. The pastor said, "I forgive you." How sad is the fact that people don't speak to each other for years, yet as they are dying, those are the people they care most about and want to be with. Why wait until that moment to ask for peace? Why not get peace while we are still living to enjoy it? Why not die in peace and harmony? This decision is up to you at the end. Only you can decide which path you want to take. My advice, take the path less traveled. That's the path most people don't take for it's too hard. If you are reading this book, then you want to take that path; that path is the path to peace and harmony.

Chapter

4

Time
With
Family And
Friends

What seemed like days was only hours away; finally all the men arrived home. The women were preparing the food for the arrival of guests. In the old days, people used to bring food over for the family of the deceased, and this is the Sunnah. However, Uncle Zakariya's family was wealthy, so they had the food catered, and told everyone not to worry about cooking. No matter what Grandma and Mom said to Aunt Khadija about relaxing and just sitting down, she refused. She didn't want to think too much and just wanted to keep herself busy.

The whole morning, tears flowed from her eyes as she thought about Rashad; his baby years, his youth, his future. She knew that she had not prepared for what just happened to them, and yet she should have. She was taught growing up as a Muslim, that this life is simply a test, and no one knows how long their term is on earth.

Allaah (SWT) said narrating from a believer at the time of Pharaoh that he said

"Oh my people, surely this worldly life is nothing but a (quick, passing) enjoyment, and certainly, the hereafter - that's the home that will last forever."
(Qur'aan 40: 39)

"My dear, you know this is the path for all of us; we have to embrace it when it comes to us. This is why I always say that we need to always be prepared for our final moment by doing more good deeds," Grandma said, as she hugged Aunt Khadija. Grandma knew how Aunt Khadija felt; she had lost one of her children when she was very young. She was aware of the feelings; how a mother feels when she loses her child.

"I know. I just wish he was ready to face Allaah (SWT). I wish that I had been a better mom to him. I wish I had taught him more about Islam. I wish that I had . . . ," said Aunt Khadija.

"I know you do," Grandma said, reassuring her. "I felt the same way when my child died so young. I felt there was so much more that I should have done. Yet, Allaah (SWT) knows we do our best with the time that we have.

Allaah knows what is in our hearts and how we feel. May He accept our repentance, and forgive our sins. May He guide us towards the path of righteousness, and shower His Mercy on us- ameen," said Grandma.

"Ameen," added Aunt Khadija.

Right then Uncle Zakariya entered the kitchen looking for his wife . . . tears flowed from his eyes. He just ran to her, and cried in her arms. Everyone else walked into the other room as they saw Uncle Zakariya and knew this was hard for him to go through alone. They knew he needed his privacy with his wife. They had been through so much in their life, and had always managed to soar through it.

Khadija tried hard to hold back her tears. She looked at her husband and said, softly, "Remember that Allaah (SWT) never gives us more than what we can handle." Uncle Zakariya nodded in agreement. He wasn't complaining about what happened. He was just sad and wished he had done more to prepare for it. A few minutes later they both walked into the living room and sat with their guests, who had come over to say their condolences.

"Do you remember the time Rashad pulled the toilet paper from the bathroom and ran around the living room with it? He wanted to see how long it was," Aunt Khadija reminisced. Everyone laughed; as they all reminisced, the sadness was lifted from their hearts and was replaced with joy. How wonderful it was to be able to look back and remember. How Great Allaah (SWT) is; He helps us understand and deal with grief, thought Grandma.

"What if we didn't have our memories? What if we didn't understand how all of this fits together? Believing in Allaah and having faith in God and the hereafter is what has kept me sane," Grandma said. Everyone nodded in agreement, pondering and acknowledging the truth behind her statement.

"Life makes more sense when you understand where you came from and what your purpose is and where you will end up. I feel sorry for all of those people who live life aimlessly and have no idea what their purpose on earth is," Mom added. Zeba drifted into her own thoughts of how true this was. Imagine living and not understanding where we came from and what our purpose is.

"Zeba, Zeba, earth calling Zeba," Sarah repeated continuously. "Where did you go?"

"I was right here, just thanking Allaah for all of His Blessings, alhamdulillaah," Zeba replied, smiling at her cousin.

"You know I won't ever forget all the events that Rashad helped out with. He tried his best to help out whenever he could, and Allaah knows best to that," Uncle Zakariya said, as he smiled.

"These moments being together in a gathering such as this, these are the memorable moments in one's life. You just don't know what you have until it's gone. So treasure them and truly be with one another. Be sincere and loving. Be honest and truthful. Have the right intentions for the sake of Allaah. Always leave people in a good state so that your last moments with them are the most memorable, and that they only make du'aa for you. SubhaanAllaah, the du'aa of a human can benefit you greatly, insha'Allaah. It is so sad that nowadays people are so corrupt that they can't be true to themselves let alone others. We need to cleanse ourselves inside out first, and only then will we be able to behave in a manner that is most befitting us," Father said, as he looked at all of the youth. He knew times were changing and these kids were lost in some ways. He could see it in their faces. "The time that you spend with great people, whether it is family, friends, or mentors, can help shed years off your learning experience. Remember my words, and you will succeed insha'Allaah. Don't take the elders for granted. Learn from their mistakes, and always seek advice from them."

Grandma entered the room and said, "How great it is to be together again and listen to all these great conversations take place." Wali smiled and nodded in acknowledgement, as he sat against the wall and thought of the last time they were all together. It was the big get together that Uncle Zakariya had for Wali and Zeba's success. Alhamdulillaah all the family was together, and everyone wanted to hear the whole story and how it happened.

"Rashad was so happy that day and he kept joking that he would be next. He wanted to prove to Uncle Zakariya that he too had what it took to be successful. What a memorable event. We stayed up for hours reciting ahadith and stories of the great Sahaabah; they were the best business people that existed. Uthman (RA) was our favorite businessman; his story is one of inspiration and beauty. It shows that you can have a balance between your deen and dunya. You never realize what wonderful moments you have with your family, until it's all taken away from you," Wali sighed.

"While most religions have emphasized good family relations, Islam has taken it to another level. A Muslim is required to be kind even to their non-Muslim relatives. Similarly they are required to be kind to even those relatives who are harsh with them," Grandpa said. Everyone was quiet, and knew Grandpa was right. "The most remarkable story of one who actually portrays this to the fullest would be Abu Bakr as-Siddique (RA). Among the many people who benefited from his generosity was a relative of his called Mistah (RA). Unfortunately Mistah (RA) became involved in the scandal about the Mother of Believers, 'Aishah (RA), which was started by the leader of the non-believers. It was a month that made everyone sad and put them through a lot of distress. Soon after, the verses of Surah Noor were revealed about her; confirming her chastity and prescribing punishment for those involved in the false accusation. This really hurt Abu Bakr as-Siddique (RA) for he was supporting Mistah, and yet Mistah was spreading lies and deceit about his daughter. It was then that he promised to discontinue his help for Mistah.

"Not too long after, Allaah revealed to the Prophet (PBUH) verses in the Qur'aan which asked him to forgive and forget and continue helping his relative, which Abu Bakr (RA) did. Think about how difficult that situation must have been. Here you are supporting someone, and they are making up lies about your family, and yet you still support them, because your Lord asked you to do it. This is the beauty of Islam," Grandpa added.

Sarah and Fatima sat quietly and looked at each other. Zeba knew they had learnt so much in the last two days from the whole family being together. Family events really can open one's eyes and mind. The growth that comes from spending a few days together is powerful, never mind the reward one gets from Allaah for keeping ties with one's kith and kin. "Good friends and good company are so hard to find these days; people who will help you grow and become a better person; people who will tell you the truth regardless of how it makes you feel; people that are sincere and truly care for you for the sake of Allaah; people who don't seek any thanks or favors in return, but want their reward from Allaah (SWT). Do you guys have any friends like that?" Zeba asked. Both Fatima and Sarah looked at each other in amazement and nodded to say no. Zeba smiled, "I don't either. So why don't we become that for each other. Are you ladies interested?"

Fatima smiled, and said, "I love it."

Sarah looked and said, "Me too."

They all smiled and hugged. "Alhamdulillaah!" they all said in a synchronized voice.

This is also a powerful topic. What do family and friends mean to you? We each have a different definition of what family and friends mean. I will tell you mine to begin with, and then I want you to think about yours. To me, my family and friends are important; however they come after my love for Allaah (SWT) and the Prophet Muhammad (PBUH). My family comes third in that category. You might ask why? It's important for one to realize that we need to love Allaah (SWT), Lord of the universe, more than we love anything else in this world. It is Allaah (SWT) Who created us and it is Him we should strive to please first and foremost. Our behaviors, our high morals, our obedience should be to Him first. If it wasn't for Him (SWT), we would not exist. People often forget that part. Many people respect and love their parents deeply, which they should, but not before they love and respect the Lord of the universe, Allaah (SWT). After Allaah (SWT), then I love the Prophet (PBUH), because he was the best of humankind created. His morals, values, and actions were the best ever seen. His example is one for the whole world to look up to. His patience, perseverance, and love were undeniable to anyone who knew him. He was truthful; he never lied, and he was known for that. A biography I recommend everyone to read. A great *hadith* to affirm what I am saying is the one that the Prophet (PBUH) said:

"Whoever possesses the following three qualities (one of which is mentioned here) has found the sweetness of faith: that Allaah and His Messenger are more beloved to him than all else..."
[Bukhari & Abu Dawood]

Everyone has different beliefs and ideas of where their family stands in the pyramid of love. As for my family, I love them deeply, and do everything I can to be close to them. Remember one thing, and that is, you cannot make everyone happy. What needs to happen is, you need to please your Lord, and with those high standards, hopefully your family will be pleased as well. If they are not, then be as nice as you can in making them understand your view. On this day, your last day to live, ask yourself "Who do I want to spend this day with?" Would you spend all day with that person? Does anyone special come to mind or maybe you wish to spend your last day with everyone you know?

For some people it is people that they have been mad at for a while now, and they want to reconnect. For others, it is their loved ones. Who is it for you? For me it would be all of my family, just one last time to see them together, and ask forgiveness from them face to face. I would want just one last time to ask them to pray for me; one last time to smile at them and love them dearly. Most importantly, I would want to remind them that death is inevitable; that death will approach all of us, and that we have to be ready for it, at all times, and learn what the purpose of our life is.

I would also like to spend as much time as possible with my kids. They are the future of the world, and I would want to tell them as much as I can before I leave; any last words of wisdom or advice that I can share with them to make them remember me. I also want them to be prepared for anything that comes their way. I want their faith to be strong in Allaah (SWT), God the Greatest, and I want them to know that we belong to Allaah (SWT) and to Him we will return.

Back to whom you will spend your time with. If the people you want to spend your time with are very dear to you, then remember them daily, as you would remember them should it be your last day. Family and friends are important, and they should be treated with importance. In order for you to impact their lives, you need to be doing it daily. We usually don't have time for our family daily, because we are so busy, but we need to find time for them. We need to love them daily, and show it to them. No matter how busy you are, remember your family daily, and remember to spend some time with them. Put them on your schedule, and make them a priority. Make time for them weekly; have a family night. For my family, Friday night is family night; every Friday evening, unless some emergency comes up, we all have pizza for dinner, and after *Isha* prayer, we all make the beds in the living room, and sleep next to each other in the living room. Meanwhile the kids play, and run around, and then we tell stories, or just talk while in bed. The kids love that so much, so much so that they look forward to Friday night. It's important to have a bond like this with your family. Of course you can choose any day of the week, but Friday is our day.

I think we all need to work on quality time with everyone in our lives; in order to achieve this we need to allocate a specific time for them. For those who are distant from you, you need to stay in touch with them over the phone, or via the email. Just take out some time every week, to be in touch with your family, and make it count. No matter how busy you are, remember they need you more, remember that. Also remember what you are teaching them; remember your actions speak louder than words. The way you act, will teach your kids and family more than what you say.

As you know many people can talk about many topics, but they never take the time to do what they say. It's putting what's most important first on your schedule that matters. We tend to put everyone else before our family, and yet it is our family who will be there for us when we need them the most. This is vital to understand. If they are the most important people in our lives, why do we think of them last? One reason for this is that most people expect their family to always be there for them, so they take them for granted. Another reason is that they are so busy with everything else, they just kind of forget their family; they are there, but not really with them. It's like quantity time, not quality time.

Everyone is around, but busy with their lives, this is what I see happening with families nowadays. This is not my definition of family–time. I think we all need to step back a moment and start to change our lives to what we really want our lives to be. Remember that we only have one chance to do what's right; one chance to make it count, and one chance to know that it made a difference. Just having dinner together with your family every night might turn your kids away from drugs, drinking and smoking. Just by talking to them before they go to bed every night might make them stay away from bad friends. You have no idea how you affect your child, unless you ask. How can your child ask you a question, if you are never home? How can your family know you love them, when you are always with your friends, and not your family? How can your parents feel your love when you don't acknowledge them anymore? Ask yourself these questions, and when your answers are in the negative, look at your situation, and know that it's not too late to change it. It's not too late to become who you want to be.

Chapter

5

My Story
Of
Change

"Pick up, pick up, you want to hear this. Where are you, Zeba?" Fatima was talking to herself, when finally Zeba's mom picked up the phone. "Assalamu-alaykum, Khala jaan (Aunty dearest), is Zeba there?" Fatima said in a rush.

"Wa-alaykum asalaam wa rahmat-Ullaah,Fatima, is that you? What's wrong, dear?" Zeba's mom asked, concerned.

"Nothing! Khala jaan. I just have some good news to share with Zeba. Is she there?"

"Yes, dear, just a sec, and I will get her for you insha'Allaah," Zeba's mom said. "Zeba, Zeba! Fatima has called for you."

"Okay, I will pick up the phone upstairs," Zeba told her mom. "Assalamu-alaykum, Fatima. How are you?" Zeba asked.

"Wa'alaykum asalaam wa rahmat-Ullaah. Alhamdulillaah, I have some awesome news, and you better say that you will come to this event, insha'Allaah. Say it, say, 'Yes, I will come, Fatima.'" Fatima said, hardly taking a breath.

Zeba couldn't help but laugh, "Insha'Allaah, if Wali or my dad will take me I will try to come . . . what is it? What is the event?" Zeba asked.

"There is a special guest speaker coming in all the way from Chicago, and she will be giving a three hour presentation about personal development and Islam; how one needs to do well in dunya (worldly affairs) and become successful for the sake of the aakhirah (hereafter). She is so inspiring and motivating. You know what's so cool about her? She wears a hijaab, like you. I can't wait until the day I put mine on. It takes guts to wear that in a non-Muslim country," Fatima said, in what seemed like one breath. Zeba smiled, she loved hearing her cousin talk about Islam.

"Insha'Allaah, you will wear it one day . . . I am definitely excited about this speaker. Email me the details so I can share it with the family, and make arrangements to come insha'Allaah," Zeba said.

"Okay, but you better be ready for a big surprise for I have never seen a sister like this in our community. She's bold and funny!" Fatima exclaimed.

Zeba laughed, "Alhamdulillaah! That is what we need in today's world; where the women are the backbone of society, but are not really out there doing what they need to do. We need strong sisters to be role models for all of us youth. Someone we can look up to and want to learn from insha'Allaah. I am so excited, I can't wait to see the email and tell everyone about it. Anyway, I have to go and pray 'Asr in about five minutes, so I will talk to you later, insha'Allaah. I love you cuz. Give my salaams to the family, and I will email you soon insha'Allaah with the verdict," Zeba said. Fatima noticed how much Zeba had grown through her life experiences; she was much more mature than all the other girls, and even more confident. Fatima loved that, as she knew Zeba was still humble as well.

"I love you too, and you give my salaams as well. I can't wait to hear from you," Fatima said, as she hung up the phone. She smiled happily, she felt so good, and couldn't wait to see this new speaker; 'Aishah Nasir; even her name sounded great,' Fatima thought.

Meanwhile Zeba ran downstairs after she made ablution, to pray in jamaa'ah with her mother and grandmother. She was so excited, but didn't want to ruin her focus on her prayer, so she decided to hold her excitement until the prayer was done. "Are we ready ladies?" Grandma asked.

"Yes!" Mom and Zeba echoed. They all stood and let Grandma lead the 'Asr prayer. SubhaanAllaah! Zeba thought; she enjoyed prayer so much, because this was the time when she asked her Lord for what she wanted. She knew that it is only Allaah (SWT) who can give her all that she needed, and that her supplications would get answered either in this world, or the hereafter. So she didn't lose out on anything when she supplicated, but she did gain a whole lot alhamdulillaah!

"Yaa Allaah, please guide my parents and family to agree for me to go to see this speaker coming up insha'Allaah. She seems awesome. I know the drive will be long for my family, but it's not every day that we get to go and see great speakers, especially women speakers," Zeba implored, as she ended her supplications. She got up and then looked at her mom and grandma, and they were still making supplications. She ran upstairs to check her email. Twenty minutes later Zeba was running down the stairs. Zeba had not only read the email, but she also 'googled' this woman, and found her website and researched more about her "Mommy jaan, Bebe jaan, are you here?" Zeba called out.

"We are in the living room, sewing," Mom replied.

Zeba ran into the living room. "Do you want to hear some amazing news?" Zeba asked.

"Sure," said Grandma. Mom nodded her head as she was finishing up the hem.

"Okay, what is this amazing news?" Mom asked.

"Well, you know why Fatima had called earlier? She called to tell me about this amazing speaker coming to San Jose, CA. This woman is an author, speaker, and Muslim life coach. Her name is 'Aishah Nasir. What's so amazing about her is that she is Muslim. She is from Pakistan, and she is so awesome! SubhaanAllaah! She is out there teaching Muslims to use their intelligence and do something great with their lives!" Zeba said, excitedly.

"Alhamdulillaah! That is wonderful! Where will she be coming to speak?" Mom asked.

"When is she going to come to our town?" asked Grandma.

"Well, she is coming to California, but not to our town, she will be at San Jose, next Friday evening, giving a presentation at the masjid after Maghrib prayer, insha'Allaah. Can we go? Mom, can we go, please?" Zeba asked. Grandma and Mom looked at each other, and knew that these types of opportunities come once in a lifetime. Mom had always wanted Zeba to have a mentor to look up to, and someone to inspire her. Although Zeba was a spectacular girl, it was always nice to see other Muslims inspire each other. Mom knew that this 'Aishah girl would probably be more inspired to meet Zeba, than Zeba meeting her. Zeba had achieved so much in such a little time, even though it was still on the hush-hush. They were dealing with the funeral, and now Wali and Zeba were getting back on track with their plans that they had for the money. "Mom, what are you thinking about?" Zeba asked.

"Nothing! Mom should we go to this event?" Mom asked Grandma.

Grandma smiled. "I think we should. Let's talk to the men about it when they come home, and then we can call Zakariya and see how it can be arranged insha'Allaah," Grandma said.

Zeba jumped up and down with excitement, shouting "Alhamdulillaah, Allaahu Akbar!"

The arrangements were made, and the family was going to San Jose to see this upcoming speaker speak. Zeba was surprised to see the whole family excited. As everyone learnt more about her, and read her biography they respected her deeply. Her story was one of great triumph; she was a single mom with 2 little children at home, and she was doing everything she could to raise them well, and yet help out the community at the same time. It had been more than a year now for Wali and Zeba since they had started working on their project and it became successful, masha'Allaah. Zeba knew deep inside that she wanted this sister to be her mentor. This sister proved through her example what can be achieved. She was different from others, for she strived hard in dunya for the sake of the aakhirah.

"Zeba, what are you thinking about?" Wali pounced in.

"The sister who we will go and see lecture. She seems really cool, and you know what, she is a practicing Muslimah. You know that is hard to find nowadays. SubhaanAllaah people are so afraid to show that they are Muslim," Zeba said.

Wali nodded in approval, "You know if people truly knew what Islam is and what a great privilege it is to represent Islam, they wouldn't be afraid. For Islam is a religion of peace, giving, tolerance, and love. Again if people only knew the roots of the religion from the time of the Prophet (PBUH), and the Companions (RA), they would not be embarrassed to say they're Muslim, they would be proud. I sure am glad that Grandma and Grandpa taught us all this while we were young."

Zeba looked at him and said, "And that we learnt to read the Qur'aan with the meaning, as when we know what it is that Allaah (SWT) is telling us, and what lessons He has taught everyone from the past, everything makes more sense. Life makes sense when the Creator explains it to you."

"You know the Qur'aan and the Sunnah are the best gifts that Allaah (SWT) gave us. If it wasn't for the example of the Prophet (PBUH), and all the other great Prophets (PBUT), I don't know whose example we would be following today. Alhamdulillaah!" Zeba said.

"Allaahu Akbar! Zeba, while I am here I wanted to talk to you about the tasks list that I had given you, do you have a progress report?" Wali smiled.

"As a matter of fact I was going to give it to you tomorrow, but we can go over it right now . . . we have twenty minutes until Maghrib prayer. Let me grab my notes," Zeba said, as she looked for the file where she had put all the paperwork. "Okay, here it is, my updates: 1. I called the attorney that Uncle Zakariya had recommended, and I told him the names we chose for our non-profits and our corporations. He searched for them in the government database, and we are clear. He is doing the paperwork on the non-profits and corporations. He will have it ready for us within another week insha'Allaah, since we had three of them. 2. Ramadhaan starts in two weeks . . . so Hajj is about two months after, insha'Allaah. We are looking around December time insha'Allaah. During Ramadhaan, all the advertisements will be out for Hajj, so I will look up all the different companies then, insha'Allaah. It's on my planner. 3. I also started organizing how I wanted the non-profits to be run. We need to start hiring some professionals to help us with this. I started searching other organizations, to see how they did it. Wali, should I put out an ad for hire?" Zeba said.

Wali smiled, he knew she was growing up . . . his little sister hiring people. "Yes, Zeba we will do that, but first we need to do a few other things. Let's talk to Mom, Dad, Grandma and Grandpa, about how we want to structure the non-profit. Also, can you talk to a non-profit expert on the structure as well? Call the president of a non-profit, maybe Islamic Relief, or the Zakat Foundation. Ask them as many questions as you can, and then just listen and take good notes. This might seem easy, but you know it's not going to be.

"Remember some of the books that you read, and how people started up their non-profits, etc. Okay, now I will tell you what I got done. I went with Dad, and opened up 5 different accounts; one for our personal use; for our parents, and the household bills, one for Grandma and Grandpa, one for Hajj, one for the non-profits, and the last one for the new business ventures we will be working on, insha'Allaah. Zeba, the next step for me is to put the business plan together and have Uncle Zakariya review it insha'Allaah.

As you know it is getting quite busy for us, especially with school and our chores, so I don't want to put too many harsh deadlines, but I do want deadlines. With everything else that's going on let's aim to get this done in two weeks insha'Allaah. Let's meet two weeks on Monday, and go over it after Fajr prayer insha'Allaah."

Friday was here and Zeba had been praying for it. She was so happy when it arrived she couldn't stop smiling. In a society where everyone only cares for concerts, musicals, and other forms of entertainment to satisfy their desires, here was a 15 year old girl who only cared for lectures by the best teachers. She had not yet met a Muslim woman up until today who she was impressed with; of course there was her mom and grandma, but not someone who was speaking, and trying to teach the youth. "What are you thinking about, Zeba?" Mom asked, knowing it had to do with tonight's event.

"Oh, Mom, I have always been so blessed to have you and Grandma in my life, but for the first time I am thinking about this amazing woman, and how she does it. You know she is widowed, and has to take care of two kids by herself, yet she still thinks about helping others. At a time when she should be asking for handouts, as most people do in her situation, she is doing the opposite. The Prophet (PBUH) said, 'The hand that gives is better than the hand that receives.' I am just amazed Mom. How often do you meet women who are extraordinary? You know Mom that Muslims are looked at as though they are terrorists, and so Muslims are too scared to be who they are. Everyone is afraid that they will be the government's new target. Yet look at her, Mom . . . she is not afraid masha'Allaah. Mom, what do you think makes her so strong?" Zeba asked.

"Well, honey, it can be many things . . . Allaah knows best. Why don't you ask her that tonight, insha'Allaah? Let's get ready for jumu'ah (Friday) prayer, insha'Allaah," Mom said. Zeba hurriedly ran upstairs to take her shower.

"We're here alhamdulillaah! Our seats are over there, and here are your seats," Wali said, as he handed Zeba the tickets for the women. The auditorium was full, and there were lots of women and youth, the men were in a separate room, where they could still hear the speaker. Zeba was surprised. She quickly scanned the room for Fatima, Sarah and Aunt Khadija. She located them sitting in the front row, with three chairs saved for Zeba, Mom, and Grandma.

"I found them," she pointed to them, and asked Grandma to lead, with Mom behind her, and Zeba behind both of them.

"Alhamdulillaah! Now that was powerful! What a great speaker! I have never seen a Muslimah with so much passion," Fatima said.

"You know she is absolutely correct in what she said; telling us to be proud of our Islam, and to show it. We are blessed to be Muslim, so why are we afraid to show it? We all want Jannah, but we don't want to work for it. I am going to do what she mentioned, and set up a goal chart with my Islamic goals, insha'Allaah. I have decided that I am going to wear the hijaab insha'Allaah," Sarah announced.

Everyone stopped walking and looked at Sarah. "Sarah, are you sure? You know hijaab isn't obligatory on *you until you reach puberty, and you're only 8 years old. Honey, hijaab isn't a joke. When a girl or woman decides to wear it, she has to respect Islam in every sense. Yet, it is very rewarding at the same time. You will get a lot of respect from Muslims and non-Muslims, because you're keeping your modesty and piety. However, remember, we do live in America, and many people are also scared of the hijaab, and the Muslim woman's image. Do you understand all that I am telling you?" Aunt Khadija asked.*

Everyone was quiet and just wanted to hear what Sarah was going to utter next. "Yes, Mom, I understand it all. I am ready to be a proud Muslim girl. I have wanted to do this for some time, and tonight was it for me - she is right! If she can do it then why can't I? I am going to do it to please Allaah (SWT), not any human. This was asked of us, and I want to obey my Lord," Sarah proclaimed, with tears in her eyes. Aunt Khadija hugged her, and told her she was so proud of her. Then everyone swarmed around her like a bee around honey and congratulated her. Zeba was crying by now.

"I am so proud of you, Sarah. There is nothing to it; you know I have been wearing my hijaab since I was 8 years old, and I feel naked without it. I am here for you if you need any support," Zeba said reassuringly. Everyone was in such a happy mood as they went out for dinner.

June 2004: I wasn't happy with how my life was. I couldn't figure out what I was missing, and why I felt so empty. I talked to many people, read many books, and thought I was doing everything I wanted correctly. I mean, I had the degrees, the houses, the husband, two beautiful children, and a great nanny. I had everything, and yet it felt as if I had nothing. I was very unsatisfied with my life, and was looking for happiness. I felt that I was really messed up in the head.

Many people would die for just one of the things that I had; maybe a great husband, or a house, the children I was blessed with, or the education I was blessed with, or even the nanny I had. I cried several days wondering what was wrong with me. Why was I so ungrateful? I had everything any woman would want, yet I wanted something else? What? I had an empty hole in my heart that nothing was filling. I knew it, and started to realize that only Allaah (SWT) can fill that void; that emptiness.

I began to seek knowledge, and my journey began. At first I was afraid to learn, as I knew that most of my life I had been following the wrong path. I knew; I felt it in me that I was on the wrong track to success; even though everyone portrayed it as success, it truly wasn't for me. All the materialistic stuff was a mirage of happiness. I kept thinking that I would be happy if I had all of these items, yet I wasn't. *Alhamdulillaah* (All Praise be to God the Greatest), what I have discovered since then is what I feel I wouldn't give up for anything. This feeling of inner peace and inner fulfillment is priceless. I am no longer curious of the hereafter, because I am aware of it. I am no longer scared of the way I am living, because now I am living as I should have been living all of my life; being truly happy with everything I have, and anything I get. I no longer want anything that is materialistic; living in simplicity and humility, is how me and my family live now. What's amazing is that if Allaah (SWT) were to take everything away from me at this point in my life, I would say *"Alhamdulillaah"*. I have full faith in Allaah (SWT), and have learnt to put all of my trust in Him.

Of course, I still work hard, but the results are up to Allaah (SWT), Lord of the universe. I won't argue why things didn't work out as I expected them to. I won't cry if I did my best, and it wasn't good enough (although there is no harm in crying, so long as it doesn't accompany words that indicate one's lack of appreciation for The Creator). If I fail, I will look at it as a lesson to learn from; behind everything I do, I know there are important lessons to be learnt, and goodness to be taken away from them. My life as you can tell transformed greatly, and has been all up rise since then. I have less in terms of the physical material things people enjoy, but I have more in my heart and soul than the whole earth can provide.

The closeness I feel towards my Lord, and the love I feel for Him is priceless. I wouldn't give it up for the world and everything in it. I have discovered true happiness, and no one can take it away from me except my Lord. I pray that my Lord helps me to maintain it, and only increases my love for Him, and my closeness to Him, for it is Him who I want to please. I know if I can please Him, I have pleased others with my character and morals, as His standards are higher than anyone else's and His Love is greater than the whole world, and everything in it.

When I meet people, I just want to be able to share with them this feeling that I have, and I want to help them achieve the same level of peace and tranquility, with Allaah's help. When I speak to you through this book, ponder over each word I say and know that there is meaning behind it; there is wisdom underlying it, and it is waiting for you to discover it. Only those who want true happiness and who want to lead a life of that sort will seek it, and it is up to God the Glorious, Allaah (SWT), to give it to whom He wills and to take it from whom He wills. When one is able to attain this sort of fulfillment in life, then the decision to treat every day as if it is your last day will be easy. For as much as one wants to succeed in this life, one wants to achieve more in the hereafter. Yet at the same time one is prepared and ready for death and the meeting with Allaah (SWT). You do your best while living, to have the best when you die and meet your Lord. You balance hope and fear.

My story is one that is possible for anyone should you truly seek the truth as I did, as long as you are truly sincere in what you want, and you know that it can only be given to you by Allaah (SWT), Lord of the universe. Only then will life take us up the path we want it to. Isn't it amazing how it can take some of us years to figure this out, while it can take others just a matter of weeks. Yet, unfortunately some of us will never discover the truth. Only if we can understand it, will it empower us. Only if we can understand it, will we be able to change. Knowledge is power only if action is taken. Knowledge is useless if we learn yet don't act upon it. It doesn't matter what we learn. Once we know, we must act according to the truth. One example of this is learning that certain foods are not good for you, and then you either quit eating those foods, or you eat less of them so it is not harmful to you. Another example is learning how to read, and yet not doing it. If you don't do it daily, you start to lose your rhythm and slow down. After a while, you start to lose what some words mean, as well as enunciate other words. Reading is one thing that should be done daily. If we take for granted what we are given, it will go away eventually as though we never possessed it. How sad is that? Think of everything you know, and many things that you learnt along the way, but didn't continue learning about . . . most likely you forgot them, right? I know, because I had learnt many things as a child, and didn't focus as much on some of them, and now I couldn't tell you how I did them.

The point of all this is to show that in order for something to be beneficial, it must be used often, this includes our brain. Muslims are required to pray five times a day. This is a great balance for us, for it allows us to do things we need to do during the day, yet we come back and remember our Lord, Allaah (SWT), and talk to Him. This is the most powerful time in my day as I know that if I need anything, only He can truly give it to me.

During those five times, I often need many things, and it is He, Allaah (SWT) Whom I ask. I know only He can truly fulfill every need I have. He might fulfill it through people, but it is He who fulfills it. Remember the Prophet (PBUH) said:

"If you ask, ask only Allaah, and if you seek help, seek it only from Allaah."[at-Tirmithi]

Chapter

6

Make
Every Moment
Count

"Sarah, do you like these colors?" Fatima asked. Fatima was showing Sarah different color hijaabs at the store. Fatima was very supportive of Sarah's decision, she wanted to help her in any way she could. She knew that one day she also wanted to wear the hijaab, and hoped that Sarah would help inspire her.

"I love the blue, and the grey one, not the red one, it's too flashy," Sarah said. Aunt Khadija had taken Sarah and Fatima shopping to help Sarah with her transition. She didn't sleep all night because she kept thinking about how Sarah was so brave, and yet she didn't have the guts to wear hijaab herself.

Aunt Khadija was a beautiful woman, and she was known for her beauty; she never thought to cover it up until she reached old age. After all that is how manyt Muslim women in the West were, they show their beauty when they are young, and behave as they wish. However, when they get to old age, then they want to go to Hajj, and from then on, cover up. Aunt Khadija began thinking about last night's conversation she had with Uncle Zakariya: "I never thought my daughter would wear the hijaab before me," Aunt Khadija told Uncle Zakariya. Uncle Zakariya was so happy for his daughter. He had already lost Rashad; he was starting to wake up to obeying Allaah (SWT). He knew life was too short, and he was going to start giving it his all.

"Masha'Allaah, I am so proud of Sarah. You know hijaab is mandatory on girls once they reach puberty; this is for their own protection. I want to read to you something that I want to write up in a card for Sarah, please tell me your thoughts on it, insha'Allaah:

"The pea is a splendid plant. It proudly displays its strong green Hijaab. It protects it from the hot and cold weather and guards it from insects. Allaah has blessed the pea with a special Hijaab, because without it, the seeds would scatter, dry up and die.

The orange keeps itself within its shiny orange Hijaab, to protect its delicious fruit. Otherwise it loses its taste too.

So are the banana, the coconut and the pomegranate. Each one has an elegant and unique Hijaab, which protects it from disease and destruction.

The jewel of the sea, the pearl, has been given a very tough and rugged Hijaab - the oyster shell. It protects it from sea animals and keeps it sparkling and shining inside.

However, the most beloved to Allaah of all His creation is the Muslim girl who wears the Hijaab. She knows it is a gift from Allaah. It protects her from harm, injury and mischief. She wears it knowing it gives her dignity, beauty and respect. So precious she can be that she hides herself beneath her Hijaab."

'O Prophet, tell your wives and daughters and the believing women that they should cast their outer garments over their bodies (when outside) so that they should be known and not molested.'
(The Qur'aan 33:59)

"I am not sure who put it together, but I received it in an email a while ago, and I saved it. I loved it, and I think it is the perfect time to share it with Sarah. What do you think, honey?" Uncle Zakariya said. He turned around from the computer to look at Aunt Khadija, and she had tears rolling down her face. She was so moved by it, that she was speechless. Uncle Zakariya went over to her, and held her as she cried.

"No one told us that the hijaab was mandatory to wear. No one told us Allaah (SWT) mentioned this in the Qur'aan for our own good. How little we really know about Islam! I am so ashamed of myself. There is so much to learn, and who knows how much time we have. Oh, Zakariya, there is so much I want to do, but where do I start?" Aunt Khadija said, as she sobbed.

"Just take it one step at a time. When you take Sarah shopping for hijaabs, you should try some on yourself. I know it will be a big change, but you can do it. It's never too late," Uncle Zakariya said.

Aunt Khadija smiled through her tears. "I feel so embarrassed, everyone will laugh at me. How will I look? I just never imagined this! It seems impossible to do," Aunt Khadija said, as she cried some more.

"Did you hear what the sister said; 'Jannah must be won! We must earn Jannah, even then it is truly through the Mercy of Allaah if we get in. We only have one chance to try to earn Jannah, and no one knows how long we have. We must do our best every day, in case it is our last day, and then pray that Allaah (SWT) accepts all that we are doing for Him and Him alone. It's all about our intentions and us trying our best, no one is perfect, all we can do is constantly change ourselves for the better, insha'Allaah.' Do you remember all that Khadija?" Uncle Zakariya said.

She nodded through her tears, "Yes. You're right, and 'Aishah was right . . . Allaah knows best. I will try my best, and take one step at a time insha'Allaah. JazaakAllaahu khayran, Zakariya for being so supportive; what would I do without you?! I know it has not been easy for you, and yet here you are wiping my tears. I will do as you suggested insha'Allaah."

"Mom, Mom! What are you thinking about? You have been sitting here for the last twenty minutes just thinking . . . is everything okay?" Sarah asked. Sarah knew it must be hard for her mom to do this, because most moms in the West did not promote the concept of hijaab for their daughters.

"Everything is fine. I was just thinking about the day when I would start wearing hijaab, insha'Allaah," Aunt Khadija replied, as tears filled up her eyes.

Sarah knew this was a struggle for her mom, "Mom, insha'Allaah you will wear it. Just make sincere du'aa to Allaah (SWT) to open your heart to accept hijaab as a blessing and not a burden. You know when I first tried it on last night; I felt so liberated alhamdulillaah. I felt like I had finally found myself - that this was me. SubhaanAllaah, please don't worry, Mom, instead just make du'aa to Allaah (SWT)," Sarah said, as she hugged Aunt Khadija. They both smiled, and held each other for what seemed like forever, but were only a few minutes.

"I love you, Sarah, and I hope that Allaah (SWT) blesses me as He has blessed you. Really, being able to wear the hijaab is an honor, and not everyone benefits from

this blessing in their life. Sarah I want you to make du'aa
for your mommy and Fatima as well. It would be an honor
to make the choice that you made last night," Aunt Khadija
said, and then they both got up to look for more hijaabs.

What does it mean to make every moment count? Treat every moment as if it is your last moment to live. How powerful is that. Live in the moment, and not in the future or in the past. Love every moment your living, by living it the best way you can. Think of your whole life in terms of moments and not years. Enjoy the moments you have, instead of thinking about moments that don't even exist, especially the moments that you have with your Lord; when you are speaking to Him, The Creator. Think about this: what if you don't live until the next prayer time? What if you don't live to see the next Ramadhaan to seek forgiveness? Make each of your prayers count as if it is your last one:

'Allaah's Messenger (PBUH) said:

"Remember death in your prayer. Verily when a man remembers death in his prayer, he is more likely to perfect his prayer. Pray the prayer of a man who does not expect to pray another prayer. And avoid every matter that would require an apology."
[Recorded by ad-Daylami (Musnadaul-Firdaw)-declared hasan by al-Albani]

Make each moment the best moment you have. If you think it will be the last moment you have, how will you behave? With death on your mind, your low desires will be killed instantly, especially for those who believe in the hereafter. The Prophet (PBUH) said:

"Frequently remember the destroyer of pleasures: death; none would remember it while in a tightness of living but it would expand it for him; and none would remember it while in an ease of living but it would tighten it for him."
[Recorded by Ibn Hibbaan, al-Bayhaqi, and others-verified to be authentic by al-Albani]

For Muslims, the thought of seeing one's Lord in any moment, can make one think twice about some of the sins one commits. Losing sight of the big picture is when we focus on our low desires. It is truly our desires that get us into trouble; from diseases to depression, all of these are outcomes of following one's low desires.

Making every moment count is when you know that life is very short and regret is very long. How many of you regret stuff that you have done in the past? Many people will answer "yes" to this question, yet they don't focus on changing themselves for the better. Change is something that takes time, and effort. No matter how many people know that, very few act on it. Unfortunately, I am here to tell you we all need to act on it. We all need to change in many areas of our lives, and we need to focus and make it happen. Change does not come from wishing for it, or imagining it. It comes from setting realistic goals to make it happen, and then accomplishing those goals. Change is needed for everyone to be able to live in the moment. The only way we can do this is by getting rid of our past which haunts us, and working on the future, but focusing on the present. I have things scheduled for the future, but I only really focus on the day to day things I need to get done. If the future arrives, you will be fine; if it doesn't you will be fine. You won't be depending on the future anymore, rather the present. This is where it gets powerful!

Many people focus so far ahead in their lives that it becomes unrealistic. Also, they don't want to die, they want to hold onto this world, for that's the only certainty they have. The only reason people don't have certainty of the hereafter is because most people don't choose to search for the truth. They feel the truth is what they already know, and what they know is enough for them.

Knowledge is vital in a human's life; without divine knowledge one cannot know one's purpose in life. Many people assume they know why they are living, but truly they have no idea; they don't know why they are here, and in reality they are afraid to know. People always want answers but they also want answers that suit their situation and desires. Unfortunately in real life that's not how it works. For Muslims, the Qur'aan is our guide, and it tells us how we should be. Prophet Muhammad (PBUH) is our example, and his teachings are what we should follow. If we all truly knew and read, we would understand at a deeper level.

Once every moment is thought about, and we understand that it is every moment that we have to pay attention to, before we act, we just might change some of our actions. People think that the little sins don't count against us, that the little things don't matter, but it is all of those little things that end up hurting us the most later on in life. The Prophet (PBUH) said:

"Beware of the belittled sins, because they gather on a person until they destroy him."
[Ahmad 1:204]

All of those little things turn into habits, which later become our character, which eventually turns into our destiny. Think about what I just said, do you want a destiny of that sort? For example, say that you yell daily, and you don't change your habit or try working on it, eventually when you're 80 years old you will still be yelling. Is that a habit that you want to keep? It's the little things that we pay no attention to that eventually creep up on us and become part of our character. The worst part is that your child too learns those habits and follows your footsteps. Can you imagine what kind of bad habits you're passing on from generation to generation? Make every moment count by changing one ***bad habit*** at a time. No one is perfect and you can't change everything overnight, but make it a habit to change one bad habit at a time. Once you have mastered one bad habit, begin at once working on another one. It's easier said than done, I know that's what you're thinking. However, if you start off with changing a small bad habit and one you can change, pretty soon you will be able to change many small habits which lead to bigger habits. As time passes, you begin to work on habits and within a short time you are able to change dramatically into the person you always dreamed to be. Of course this does not happen overnight, and you do need to work on it a little every day. It's easier said than done, is what most people say, however, they don't even try to do it. They don't even attempt to change themselves or their lives. People think they can't do it, or it's too difficult. How can you know if something is too difficult if you haven't even tried it? It is vitally important to remember that if it was our last day to live we would have all of these big expectations from ourselves, yet right now we don't choose to even try to change a tiny bit of ourselves. Remember, where there is a will there is a way!

This is the one chance we have to change, and yet we don't take it. We don't even try. Do you know what's stopping most people from taking a chance to change and becoming a better person? It is the mere fact that they don't think of death as being so close to them. They feel that death is a far off distant thing, and that they have a long time to live. People love the worldly life so much, that death is hated by them. For believers, they don't fear anything except their Lord, Allaah (SWT), yet they have this great love for Allaah (SWT). They are those who will work hard in this life to please Allaah (SWT), yet they will be ready to embrace death as it comes to them. Mostly, people of this sort have made amends with the past, and asked for forgiveness. They are trying their best to follow the right path, and change themselves for the sake of Allaah (SWT). They wish to please Allaah (SWT), with all of their actions and words. This doesn't guarantee anyone *jannah* (paradise), however it does show Allaah (SWT) that one of His slaves is sorry, and is repenting. Now the human hopes for the Mercy of Allaah (SWT) to be bestowed upon him. It is only through His Mercy that we are able to attain goodness and be guided.

Again I come back to reminding myself and you that death is much closer to us than we can imagine. Every day that we wake up we are one day closer to death. We have one day less to make a decision and change for the best. We see with our own eyes that death comes to everyone, and it will be a surprise coming to us as well. We won't know where it's coming from or how we will die, but we know it is coming. Ponder over this and see what you think:

One Way Ticket to the Underground
(Written by Mohamed Chetty)

"When we are leaving this world for the next one, it shall be like a trip to another country; where details of that country won't be found in glamorous travel brochures but in the Noble Qur'aan and the hadiths; where our plane won't be British Airways, Gulf Air or American Airlines but Air Janaazah.

Where our luggage won't be the allowed 23 kgs but our deeds no matter how heavy they weigh. You don't pay for excess luggage. They are carried free of charge, with your Creator's compliment. Where our dress won't be a Pierre Cardin suit or the like but the white cotton shroud, where our perfume won't be Chanel, Paco Rabane, but the camphor and attar.

Where our passports won't be British, French or American, but Al-Islam. Where our visa won't be the 6 months leave to stay or else but the "Laa 'Ilaaha Illallaah." Where the airhostess won't be gorgeous females but Isra'iil and its like; where the in-flight services won't be firstclass or economy but a piece of beautifully scented or foul smelling cloth.

Where our place of destination won't be Heathrow Terminal one or Jeddah International Terminal but the graveyard. Where our waiting lounge won't be nice carpeted and air-conditioned rooms but the 6 feet deep gloomy grave. Where the Immigration Officer won't be Her Majesty's officers but Munkar and Nakir.

They only check out whether you deserve the place you yearn to go. Where there is no need for Customs Officers or detectors. Where the transit airport will be Al Barzakh. Where our final place of destination will be either the Garden under which rivers flow or Hell Fire. This trip does not come with a price tag. It is free of charge. So your savings would not come handy. This flight can never be hijacked so do not worry about terrorists.

Food won't be served on this flight so do not worry about your allergies or whether the food is halaal. Do not worry about legroom; you won't need it, as your legs will become things of the past. Do not worry about delays. This flight is always punctual; it arrives and leaves on time. Do not worry about the in-flight entertainment program because you would have lost all your sense of joy. Do not worry about booking this trip, it has already been booked the day you became a fetus in your mother's womb.

Ah! At last good news! Do not worry about who will be sitting next to you. You will have the luxury of being the only passenger. So enjoy it while you can. If only you can! One small snag though, this trip comes with no warning - Are you prepared?"

My dear readers, if death is inescapable, isn't it time to change while we still have time to do it? Allaah (SWT) is giving us one more chance everyday to come closer to Him, yet we are not taking it. I want you to ponder over this next question, and think about the answer before you continue reading the next part of this book. If you were to die right now, do you think Allaah (SWT), God the Greatest, will be happy with you? Please think deeply about this question, and then write the answer down, and reflect on it.

90% of people say "No" to this question, and yet they don't change. They complain that it is too hard, that they were taught the wrong way, and that their parents are to blame. It's time for us to take account for ourselves. If you can read this book, then you're old enough to know it's time to change, and the time is right NOW! Let's make it happen. No more excuses, no more blaming everyone else.

Chapter

7

Making Today A Better Day

"What a day! Alhamdulillaah!" said Wali.

"What happened?" asked Zeba.

Wali had just come home, and ran upstairs to find Zeba. "Well, like you I finished the business plan a few days ago, and today was my meeting with Uncle Zakariya. He thought it was awesome alhamdulillaah! Do you want to hear it?" Wali was so excited, that he couldn't hold his excitement any longer.

"Yes, I want to know which business we will start with first, insha'Allaah," Zeba replied.

"After lots of research and thinking, do you remember the idea of the teaching robot that I gave before we began working on the 'Interactive Computer'?" Wali asked.

"Yes," said Zeba.

"Well that is what I have put a business plan together for. I have done a lot of research on it, and I didn't want to bother you with it, because of all the work you have on your plate . . . what do you think?" Wali asked.

"I love the idea! The only question is, is there a market for this?" Zeba asked.

"That is the best part; the home schooling industry is increasing by 7% each year . . . it is a billion dollar industry as we speak. Think about it, how many parents would love to home school their kids, but don't have the time, or the skills? What if this teaching robot, can solve their problems insha'Allaah? What if it could explain subjects, depending on the grade level? The details are in the business plan. Are you starting to see the vision behind this invention, Zeba?" Wali asked.

"Yes, I am! It sounds so exciting, masha'Allaah!" Zeba replied enthusiastically.

"Alhamdulillaah! Okay, before we go over the details and how we should work on this project as I have devised it and researched it, I want to hear about the non-profit you were working on," Wali said.

"Alhamdulillaah, I spoke to the president of Zakat Foundation, and he was very helpful masha'Allaah. Do you know how much work goes into a non-profit? SubhaanAllaah, it is not as easy as it looks, Wali! As I was *asking him all of these questions, an idea came to me; why not just partner up with a big non-profit who is doing a lot of what we want to do, donate to them, and get on board with them," Zeba asked. Wali listened very carefully to all Zeba had just said. She was right he thought, there wasn't enough time or manpower for them to do it all by themselves. Non-profits would also take a lot of time and effort insha'Allaah.*

"That sounds like a great idea, but the question is which non-profit will we partner up with, insha'Allaah? Their goals and values have to align with ours . . . have you seen any organizations that you really like, and would want us to work with, Zeba?" Wali asked.

Zeba smiled, "I knew you were going to ask that question. Yes, I did. I liked this organization very much; The Zakat Foundation." Wali smiled as he was familiar with them, for in the past his family had donated to them.

"Okay, so what I think you should do next is interview them, to see if we want to partner up with them insha'Allaah. This move could be great for us, insha'Allaah as it will save us a lot of time, and research insha'Allaah," Wali said.

"Also it will be fun just to jump in and be part of the actual helping, instead of putting it together and organizing it insha'Allaah. I am so excited, insha'Allaah this is what I have been dreaming about since we started the business, the day we can give and make a difference for the sake of Allaah (SWT)," Zeba added.

Dad was walking by and he overhead his teens talking. "Zeba, Wali, can I talk to you for a few minutes?" Dad asked.

"Sure, Dad, what's on your mind?" asked Wali.

"I just overhead you two, and masha'Allaah I am so proud of you both, may Allaah (SWT) give you even more success- ameen! One thing I just want to remind you of is your intention. Sometimes we start off doing things with good intentions, but then Satan drives us other ways. Make sure you purify your intentions as often as you can, for the sake of Allaah (SWT), this will be better for you:

'The Prophet (PBUH) said: "Actions are (judged) by motives (niyyah), so each man will have what he intended. Thus, he whose migration (hijrah) was to Allaah and His Messenger, his migration is to Allaah and His Messenger; but he whose migration was for some worldly thing he might gain, or for a wife he might marry, his migration is to that for which he migrated."'
(Bukhari & Muslim)

"I would love it if Allaah (SWT) accepts everything you guys do for His sake only, so always make sure that your intentions are solely for Allaah (SWT)," Dad advised.

Zeba and Wali were silent as they listened to the hadith, and contemplated over its meaning. "You're right, Dad. Insha'Allaah we will definitely remember those words . . . if we forget Dad please remind us . . . we are human, and full of error. I love you, Dad. I love you for always paying attention to us, when we aren't," Zeba said as she leaned over and kissed her dad on his forehead. Since Zeba was a little girl her dad always kissed her on her forehead, and Zeba would kiss her dad back on his forehead. It was a sign of affection between them.

"Dad, we are just making today a better day for anyone we can help insha'Allaah. You know that everything we are doing is to please Allaah (SWT); we need your du'aas always, as well as your guidance. Zeba and I want to discuss all matters with the family, insha'Allaah, and we want to get feedback from all the elders," Wali said, as he hugged his dad. He knew that if it wasn't for his parent's full support, he and Zeba would not be doing what they were doing. Of course everything is what Allaah (SWT) Wills, but his family gave them the freedom to be home schooled and creative, so that they can do more than the average person, insha'Allaah. "Okay, let's go downstairs and get ready for Maghrib prayer, and then dinner, insha'Allaah. We can discuss this with everyone during dinner, insha'Allaah," Wali said. They all got up to head downstairs.

M any times we want to achieve certain things, but we don't know how to do it. Many times we imagine the perfect day in our minds and heart, but we can't figure out how to attain it. Many times we pray for better days to come, yet we don't have enough faith that this will happen. Making a better day today is not impossible, nor is it so far that you can't reach it. It is actually reachable if you truly desire it.

Making a better day should begin with praying the five prayers daily. The five prayers help us walk the straight path, and if we are about to make a bad choice in anything, our prayer will make us think twice about it. I know this, for many times it has helped me. We are human and Satan is trying to misguide us at all times; he always wants to misguide us so we can accompany him to hell. The prayers we offer help us divert our attention back to what is good, and most importantly the prayers help us to connect with Allaah (SWT). It is only Allaah (SWT) who guides us or allows us to be misguided. It is only Allaah (SWT) who can help us with our trials; whether it is trying to be patient with one's child or trying to pass a test in school. It is only Allaah (SWT) that can help us, yet some people are slow to realize this. They think they themselves are capable of achieving whatever they desire, and that they alone achieve it. This is impossible! If one should seek the truth and find out why they were created, they would know better; they would know that they can't do anything without the Will of Allaah (SWT)- *Laa hawla wa laa quwwata 'illaa billaah* (There is no movement nor power except by Allaah's Will).

In addition to the above which is an obligatory act, making a better day should include voluntary worship such as reciting the Qur'aan every day. This alone brings in so much *barakah* (blessing) and joy in a day that it's beyond words to explain it. Imagine reading the Words of Allaah (SWT) and then realizing many things as you read those empowering words and ponder over them. Imagine that if today is your last day you started if off with Allaah (SWT), and if you die, it ended by you returning to Him. I know many people who recite the Qur'aan daily, and their day is not the same if they don't recite it; they are saddened, and have more issues than usual. This is a powerful recipe, and the Prophet (PBUH) is our greatest example, for that is how he led his life. If you want a better day, start off with salaah (prayer) and then make time to recite the Qur'aan every day, insha'Allaah.

The second voluntary ingredient that I will recommend is praying *tahajjud* (Night prayer). *SubhaanAllaah, tahajjud* prayer is so different from the whole day's prayers, simply because it is you voluntarily getting up in the night, leaving the comfort of your bed, to please Allaah (SWT). It's more peaceful and quiet. You really connect with your Lord, as long as you're sincere and trying to focus while praying. The greatest thing I learnt was that while one is praying, one should make sure that one prays for things that are good and pleasing to Allaah (SWT). If you don't know what's good or bad for you, then Allaah (SWT) will decide that for you. If He thinks something is bad for you, then He will not answer that supplication. Instead one should wait patiently and understand that we as humans don't know what is good for us and what is bad for us, only Allaah (SWT), God the Greatest, knows all of this. We have to accept the fact that we need to work hard, and do our best, but leave the rest up to Allaah (SWT). The Prophet (PBUH) said:

"There is no person who asks Allaah for anything except that Allaah gives it to him, or keeps away from him a similar evil, as long as he does not ask for something evil or for breaking the ties of kinship."
[at-Tirmidhi]

Tahajjud prayer is a time when Allaah SWT is closest to the creation. The Prophet (PBUH) said:
"Our Lord- all Glory and Praise be to Him - descends down (not to be taken literally) in the last third of the night to the lowest heaven, and He says: 'Who is there that is making du'aa, so that I can respond to him? Who is there that is asking me, so that I can give him? Who is there that is seeking my forgiveness, so that I can forgive him?"
[Bukhari & Muslim]

"It is during the prostration that the servant is closest to Allaah (SWT)."
(Recorded by Muslim and others)

Making a better day should involve you making supplication the moment that you wake up. You say your *du'aa* (supplication), and connect with Allaah (SWT) as soon as you open your eyes:

'Alhamdu lillaahil-ladhee 'ahyaanaa ba'da maa 'amaatanaa wa'ilayhin-nushoor (Praise be to Allaah Who gives us life after He has caused us to die and to Him is the return).'
[Bukhari]

Imagine starting the day with the blessings of your Lord, Allaah (SWT) - how powerful is that - that alone can help make your day great. Those words show you that you are truly dependent on Allaah (SWT), and that you realize your dependence and that you are asking for His blessings.

Making a better day should always begin with a positive mental attitude - believe it's going to be a great day, regardless of what happens today. You should tell yourself that 'regardless of what tests are thrown my way, I will appreciate and respect all that was given to me today, and that no matter what happens, I will be patient and know that everything is happening for a reason. Nothing happens without Allaah (SWT) allowing it to happen' and we should remember that Allaah SWT tells us in the Qur'aan:

"And no calamity strikes except by Allaah's Permission."
(The Qur'aan 64:11)

The Prophet (PBUH) elaborated on the above concept and said:

"Be aware that if the whole of mankind gathered together in order to do something to help you, they would only be able to do something for you which Allaah had already ordained for you. Likewise, if the whole of mankind gathered together to harm you, they would only be able to do something to harm you, which Allaah had already written to happen to you."
[at-Tirmidhi]

Once we are aware of this we are more apt to accept all that happens to us. It makes us more patient and humble. It is so empowering that just one's attitude can make so much of a difference when one is hit with a calamity. If you try to keep up your attitude with what it is supposed to be like at all times, then you are better able to cope with anything that is thrown at you. Amazingly this is true, test it. You just have to be consistent with your attitude. You have to work on your attitude daily, and try to think of all the blessings that you have been blessed with, instead of what you don't have. Ibn Abi'd-Dunyâ said:

"It was narrated to me that some scholars said: 'The scholar should praise Allâh for having deprived him of the luxuries of this life, in the same way that he should praise Him for what He has bestowed upon him. How can you compare the blessings and luxuries for which he will be accountable to the deprivation of luxuries which is a relief from being tested, and which keeps his mind free to worship and remember Allâh? So he should give thanks to Allâh for all of that."
[Taken from "Uddat as-Sâbireen wa Dhâkirat ash-Shâkireen (Have you thanked Allaah?) By Imâm Ibn Qayyim al-Jawziyyah]

People say that positive thinking doesn't help, and it's all just a joke. I beg to differ. I feel like positive thinking is the beginning process of the long journey of success. Think of it this way, if you smile, your mood starts to be happier. Success is given to some while not to others, but it really depends on your definition of success. Allaah (SWT) says in the Qur'aan:

"Allaah has promised the believers - men and women, - Gardens under which rivers flow to dwell therein forever, and beautiful mansions in Gardens of 'Adn (Eden Paradise). But the greatest bliss is the Good Pleasure of Allaah. That is the supreme success."(The Qur'aan 9:72)

We all have something special from Allaah (SWT), all we need to do is discover it and focus on it. It doesn't matter if you're poor, rich, have all of your limbs, or have some of them.

Allaah (SWT) has blessed all of us in one way or another; we just need to realize it, respect it, and appreciate it.

Having a positive mental attitude requires that we use positive language as opposed to negative language. This is very hard for people to do, but we have to keep trying until we make a habit out of it. We have to be consistent and remember that what we think will become our words and our words affect our actions. We have to remember that our words will impact those around us tremendously; if we use negative words we will soon regret what we said. If on the other hand we use positive words, we will soon wish we had said much more of it. Does our language matter? Absolutely! Words and the way they are spoken are powerful tools to how we will react in any situation. Just by using certain vocabulary one is able to empower their day, as opposed to being defeated by their day. A word I highly recommend people use whenever they talk about doing something in the future is "*Insha'Allaah*" (If Allaah Wills):

"And never say of anything, "I shall do such and such thing tomorrow. Except (with the saying), "If Allaah wills!"
(The Qur'aan 18:23-24)

This means that you will try your best, and if Allaah (SWT) Wills, you can do it, and if He does not Will then you cannot do it, even if you tried your best. Either way you're happy, for you acknowledge your own limitations and accept that all power belongs to Allaah (SWT); that Allaah knows best as to what is good for you and what is not good for you, as mentioned earlier. What we often forget is that matters are decreed for us the way Allaah (SWT) has ordered it to be, and that we can't change that even if we tried. Once we are able to accept whatever comes our way, then we will have the right attitude and words to go along with it - this is a vital point to understand – when I discovered this one piece of information my whole way of thinking changed dramatically. It's so sad how only few people actually have knowledge of why we were created and what our capabilities are. The more one discovers the purpose of existence, the more one can understand how we can train ourselves to be who we should be. If we don't know why we are here, then how will we know how to react while we are here? Think about it - can we train someone to be a computer specialist if they applied for the position of a dietician?

Making a better day means having no grudges in one's heart. It means that you are at peace with everyone you know. You are happy with what is going on in your life. If you want more, you have to work hard to obtain it. If you don't, you just go along with your life as you are. However, one small fact to note is that sometimes you have to accept to be uncomfortable in order to be comfortable in the long run. If you choose to have an easy going life right now, no pressure, then you will have pressure later in your life. It's your choice. Choices are what make us or break us. I always tell people life doesn't pass anyone by without hardships and troubles. It's just how one reacts to their troubles and hardships that identifies if they want more out of life, or if they will settle with what they got; either choice you make is fine. Only Allaah (SWT) knows who will be granted paradise and who will not. However, as a believer I have to do my best in everything I do, in hopes of attaining paradise; which means I have to strive in *dunya* (world) for the sake of the hereafter. That starts with eliminating some of the grudges or hatred in your heart for others. If anything you feel sorry for those who have hatred, envy, jealousy, and all those feelings that Satan wants one to have, for all these feelings do is, they consume up one's energy and time as well as one's good deeds. The Prophet PBUH said:

"Jealousy eats away good deeds, just as fire eats away firewood, and giving charity extinguishes sins just as water extinguishes fire."[Ibn Majah]

I have learnt a great lesson from the Prophet (PBUH); to be patient and to have faith in Allaah (SWT). Making a better day means to wake up and make sure that every day you do one additional act of kindness. It doesn't matter how big or small it is, just make the effort to do one extra act of kindness every day. The Prophet (PBUH) said:

"Do not disdain a good deed, (no matter how small it may seem) even if it is your meeting with your (Muslim) brother with a cheerful face."
[Muslim]

You don't know which good act will be the one that will help you in the hereafter. The Prophet (PBUH) said:

"A man saw a dog eating mud from (the severity of) thirst. So, that man took a shoe (and filled it) with water and kept on pouring the water for the dog till it quenched its thirst. So Allaah approved of his deed and made him to enter Paradise."
[Bukhari]

You don't know what one small act of charity can do for the other person; it can make some one's day, and make you feel good, that you're doing what you're supposed to do. Again the deed can be just to spend an hour with your kids without any interruptions, or taking the garbage out. It can be anything, just as long as you do something nice for someone else. Amazingly some of these acts of niceness start to become embedded in your normal routine as life goes on. How powerful is that! This is just the beginning of making a difference. As humans we will never be perfect, but striving to be the best that we can be, is good enough.

Making a better day means envisioning a day that you love; a day that you feel is the best day that you can have, because you have done your best that day. It starts out with what is most important, to lesser and lesser importance. For example, I want to focus everyday of mine with the five daily prayers, reciting the Qur'aan, *tahajjud* prayer, Duha prayer, etc; these are the most important things that I have to do daily. In addition to this is teaching my kids, home schooling, and then it is running my business. *Alhamdulillaah*, I usually get to manage it all pretty well. The day which I can achieve this schedule is by far my perfect day *masha'Allaah*. However, I have had to sit down many times and think about what the most important things that had to get done daily were, for me. *SubhaanAllaah!* Allaah (SWT) helped me realize what is most important, and what will benefit me the most daily. Four years ago I would have given you a totally different schedule to this. As time goes and we learn and grow, we start to realize that our priorities change substantially to what really counts. Most people, if you notice, are a slave to this world, and they are because of the decisions that they themselves made. We all have choices, it's up to us to make the choices which will benefit us the most, and the only way we can discover what decisions are best for us, is by finding out our purpose in life. For the true believers it is, loving Allaah (SWT) the most, that they would give up all of their low desires and just desire their Lord to be pleased with them. I guarantee you that if you do all that you're supposed to be doing, and have your Lord pleased with you; others will definitely be pleased with you in the long run. Why? Simply because your morals, integrity, values have to be at a high level to please Allaah (SWT). If they are at that level, then most of mankind will automatically be pleased with your character.

The Prophet (PBUH) said:

"Indeed, when Allaah loves a (good) person, He calls to Jibreel (AS), "I love so-and so, so love him." Jibreel loves him and calls out in the heavens, "Allaah loves so-and so, so love him." The angels of the heavens love him, and acceptance is laid down for him on earth. And when Allaah dislikes a (bad) person, He calls to Jibreel, "I hate so-and so, so hate him." Jibreel then hates him and calls out in the heavens, "Allaah hates so-and so, so hate him." The angels of the heavens hate him, and hatred is laid down for him on earth." ***[Muslim]***

Chapter

8

Understanding Yourself

"Khadija, what are you doing in the room? You have been in there for more than an hour. Is everything okay?" Uncle Zakariya called out.

"Just a moment, I will be out in a minute, just finishing up," Aunt Khadija replied. Uncle Zakariya went back to reading the 'Wall Street Journal'; every week he read the 'Wall Street Journal' to learn what was happening with businesses, what was booming, and what was not. Business is an amazing thing, it can be hot one day, and out of business the next day. Uncle Zakariya loved learning, and wished that it was Rashad who took over his businesses one day, but Allaah knows best. "Okay, I am done! What do you think?" Aunt Khadija asked.

"Masha'Allaah, you look stunning!" Uncle Zakariya said. Aunt Khadija had just walked in with a cloak (abaya) and a matching hijaab. This was the first time Uncle Zakariya had seen her this way. "I must say that you look like a pearl inside an oyster shell. What is amazing is that you're still so beautiful, just in a more reserved way," Uncle Zakariya said, as he got up to hug his wife.

Aunt Khadija smiled bashfully. "I like it. I think I am ready to uncover who I am. I have been ignoring this for a long time, trying to understand who I am. These past two weeks I have been praying and asking Allaah (SWT) to help me find who I am, and I feel this is me. I used to think my head would look too big in hijaab, and that I will look fat in an Abaya! All the insecurity questions women ask themselves, but as I looked in the mirror I realized I look thinner in the abaya, and the hijaab is comfortable. I also like the fact they match. More than anything I like the fact that I can be distinguished as a Muslim woman. That is who I am, and that is what I am proud of, so why hide it, right?" Aunt Khadija said. Uncle Zakariya was in utter silence; he was amazed at how his wife spoke. She spoke with such strength in her voice, and such conviction in discovering her identity.

"You can't be wrong," Uncle Zakariya finally said. Those were Aunt Khadija's favorite words.

She smiled and said, "You always know when to say the right thing, don't you?" Uncle Zakariya just watching her this whole time, had tears in his eyes now.

"Can I call Fatima and Sarah to come and see you?" Uncle Zakariya asked.

"Yes, please, I will go into the closet, and then when they come, I will come out," Aunt Khadija giggled.

"Fatima, Sarah, please come to our room, your mom and I have something we want to share with you, insha'Allaah!" Uncle Zakariya called out, from his bedroom door.

"Coming, Daddy jaan," both girls echoed. What seemed like forever was only minutes away, when Fatima and Sarah entered the room. They were curious to know what they would be hearing from their mom and dad.

"Where is Mom?" Sarah asked.

"Khadija, the girls are both here. Please come out!" Uncle Zakariya said.

Aunt Khadija opened the door and slowly walked out, "Well, what do you girls think of your Mom's new look?" Aunt Khadija asked as she gave them a little twirl.

Sarah had tears in her eyes and ran to hug her mom, "I love it Mom! I just love it! You look so beautiful!" she cried.

Fatima smiled and went to her mom as well, "I am just shocked Mom, in a good way of course. You truly are glowing wearing the hijaab masha'Allaah. There is this light on your face that I can't describe. May Allaah (SWT) guide me as well, and help me discover who I truly am," Fatima said, as she hugged her mom too. All three of them were in tears by now, tears of joy.

"I have always wished for this; that we live our lives the way the Prophet (PBUH) instructed us to, but I haven't had the guts to change who I was, therefore, I never told any of you to do it. I was scared and worried about what people would think, therefore, I hid under the workload I piled on top of myself. This is so much my fault. This is why I love Wali and Zeba very much, because they obey Allaah (SWT) as youth, and I wish that I had done it from such a young age. I respect them a lot, for they are proud of their

Muslim identity, and their most important goal in life is to please Allaah (SWT) first and foremost. What's sad is that Rashad never experienced any of this. SubhaanAllaah, Allaah knows best. It is too late for him, but we need to change before it is too late for us as well, insha'Allaah. Nobody knows how long this life will be, so we need to act on it as soon as possible, or else we will have regrets," Uncle Zakariya said.

His wife and daughters were all sitting on the bed, listening to him. "You're right, Dad! I have so much that I already regret and wished had never taken place. I agree 100%, and am thinking we should go to the masjid every Friday night for halaqahs insha'Allaah. We should also pray in jamaa'ah when we are together. If it is okay with everyone, can we sit together every Saturday morning for one hour and listen to a new lecture on CD? I have found them so useful," Sarah said, excitedly.

"I love the idea, and I can't wait to learn more insha'Allaah," Fatima replied.

Uncle Zakariya looked at Aunt Khadija and smiled, and they both said, "Alhamdulillaah!"

This chapter is all about understanding who you are. Most of us are lost and have no idea who we really are, yet no one knows us better than our Lord, Allaah (SWT). After Him, we know ourselves best. We know what goes on in our minds, in our inner selves, our thoughts, our feelings, and our emotions. We know when we are lying and when we are telling the truth. We know when we are truly happy and when we are sad. We know when we want to do something and we know when we hate to do something. It's amazing how well we know ourselves once we start to pay attention to ourselves. We know that our behavior is a reflection of our thoughts. We know that our manners and attitude are a reflection of what our parents taught us early on, or what they didn't teach us. What we don't know is how we can change ourselves into becoming better human beings. What we don't know is what skills are necessary for us to possess to make those changes stick with us. What we don't know is where all the answers lie. Some of you might say that you do know; yet you are just not changing for some reason or another. I am here to tell you that whether you know or don't know, it is time to truly understand yourself, and bring your soul to peace while living in this world.

In order for this peace to come to you, to truly understand your mind, body and soul, you will have to do some work. I suggest that you take a sheet of paper and fold it into half. Once you have done that, begin writing on half the page who you are right now. On the left hand side of the paper list all the characteristics and habits that you have. Then on the right hand side list all of the characteristics and habits that you desire to obtain. I will give you some examples here so that you understand better:

Left Hand Side	Right Hand Side
• I talk on the phone too much.	I will talk on the phone only when it is something important to discuss.
• I watch too much TV	I will only watch 4 hours of TV a week
• When I get upset I yell	I will make wudhu

- I am not praying all of my 5 prayers
- I obey my parents
- I procrastinate in my work

I will pray all 5 prayers. insha'Allaah

I can talk to my cousins whom I never speak to.

I need to take a class on time management.

I hope that you can see from the example listed above that what you are, and who you want to be is very different. What needs to happen now is that you need to begin to develop a system to help you get to who you want to be. Deep down inside you want to better understand yourself, *insha'Allaah* (If Allaah Wills). What makes you angry? Is that a good enough reason to be angry? Do you want to change that habit? What makes you excited to wake up every morning? What is it that makes you want to live? What is it that excites you? Are they good things to do or bad things to do? If they are bad, what are the consequences if you don't change them? If they are good things to do, how can you improve on them? You know there is always room for improvement, *insha'Allaah*. I will give you an example of a good thing and a bad thing. A good thing would be; you're a parent, and you want to be the best parent out there, *insha'Allaah. Alhamdulillaah* your childhood was good, but you want to give your children a better childhood; one they remember, *insha'Allaah*. You know that it is their childhood that will shape them into the type of adult they turn out to be, *insha'Allaah*. For the sake of Allaah (SWT), you want to do your job as best as you can, so that you have no regrets *insha'Allaah* at the end. What you can do is look at all the areas you want to improve on; one example would be to listen to your children more when they talk, instead of ignoring them and treating them as though everything else is more important than them. You decide that every time your child talks to you, you will look at him/her, and give your child that minute to speak, and just nod your head to show that you're listening to them. After they are done, you can go back to whatever it is that you were working on. This is the start to becoming a better parent, *insha'Allaah*.

I will give you a personal example of something bad that needs to change before it is too late, *insha'Allaah*. This is a personal story about me, to hopefully help you understand my message, *insha'Allaah*; when I was younger and I didn't pray my prayers, I would act like nothing happened. In my mind Satan was always saying, *"It's okay if you miss your prayers, you're young, and you can do it when you get older. You can do it later. Everyone else is missing them too. You're a good person inside, you have a good heart, and Allaah only looks at your heart; He will forgive you. He is the Most Merciful."* With all these thoughts in my mind, one prayer after another was missed, *astaghfirullaah* (I seek forgiveness from Allaah). I knew very little about the importance of prayers and why it is established for us! Prayer has so many benefits; for me, once I learned about them I regretted missing all those prayers. For example:

The Prophet (PBUH) said,

"Five (daily) prayers and from one Friday prayer to the (next) Friday prayer, and from Ramadan to Ramadan are expiations for the (sins) committed in between (their intervals) provided one shuns the major sins."
[Muslim & Tirmidhi]

In a *Hadith Qudsi* (Prophet quoting Allaah), 'The Prophet (PBUH) said,

"Out of all the ways through which My servant gets closer to Me salaah is the dearest to Me."
(Bukhari)

'The Prophet (PBUH) said,
"Du'aa (asking) is the essence of worship." (Tirmizi) (We should always make our *du'aa* to Allaah (SWT) with the intention that whatever we are asking for will be granted *insha'Allaah* (If Allaah Wills)).

A believer who makes *du'aa* (supplication to God) receives one of three things:
1. Either he will quickly have his du'aa answered,
2. Or he will get the reward in the Hereafter,
3. Or something bad will be prevented from him equal to the value of his *du'aa* (so no *du'aa* is ever wasted).

I made a vow to pray always *insha'Allaah* (If Allaah Wills), and to make as much *du'aa* (supplication to Allaah) as I can, for whatever I wanted, *insha'Allaah*.

Understanding yourself usually leads to pondering over whom it is that you want to become, and what it is that you want to discover in this life? Think about it, do we really know who we are? Do we really know what our purpose in this life is? Do we really understand what makes us happy, and what makes us sad? Lastly, does all of this fit in with obeying our Creator? I realized that in order for me to be truly happy, and understand who I am, I need to be following the path that was best for me. After so much research and studying; I realized that that path was none other than that which was given to us by Allaah (SWT). I realized that everything that the Prophet (PBUH) said to us, and taught us was in sync with who I wanted to be, and with what truly made me happy, *Allaahu Akbar* (Allaah is the Greatest)!

I want you to ask yourself some questions now:

- Do I know who I am?
- Do I know what I want?
- Do I know where I am headed with firm determination?
- Or, am I lost?
- Am I following the crowd blindly, just to please everyone?
- Do I believe in anything because of the truth, or is it because that is what I was told to believe?

Questions like these and many more will open your mind to understanding yourself better, and what your purpose in life is. Once you can align yourself truly to who you want to be, then you have to start taking action to become that person *insha'Allaah*. You can't just imagine that you're praying five times a day; you need to get up and do it. You can't just imagine that you're treating people with respect, but then you yell at them. You have to hold yourself back, listen to them, and then think and ponder before you answer *insha'Allaah*. You can't just imagine that you're going to manage your time to be more productive, you must make a schedule and eliminate the things that are wasting your valuable time.

Understanding yourself is truly the most beneficial thing to do. Once you can understand who you are, and where you are headed, you will be at peace *insha'Allaah*. You won't have regrets, and you will enjoy life no matter what it brings you, *insha'Allaah*; for Muslims that involves belief in the *Qadr* (The Divine Decree) of Allaah (SWT); that Allaah (SWT) has decreed certain things to be as they are, and all we should do is our best, but it is Allaah (SWT) who is in control of our destiny. Think about it, we don't control when we are born, when we will die, the weather conditions, etc. All we can do is try our best, and then be happy with whichever route Allaah (SWT) guides us to. It is not an easy journey to understand oneself; it is a journey that one never stops learning from. Only through learning can one truly change who they are to what they want to be *insha'Allaah*. Millions if not more, never get to this point in their lives. People ignore who they are, and live life as others want them to live it, and follow the crowds blindly. Before it is too late, discover who you truly are, and live as that person; full of happiness, honesty, and most importantly obeying the Laws of your Creator. When we are able to do this, then and only then will we have truly understood ourselves.

Bonus Chapter:

A

Story

To

Remember

Two men, both seriously ill . . .(unknown)

Two men, both seriously ill, occupied the same hospital room. One man was allowed to sit up in his bed for an hour each afternoon to help drain the fluid from his lungs. His bed was next to the room's only window. The other man had to spend all his time flat on his back.

The men talked for hours on end. They spoke of their wives and families, their homes, their jobs, their involvement in the military service, where they had been on vacation.

Every afternoon when the man in the bed by the window could sit up, he would pass the time by describing to his roommate all the things he could see outside the window.

The man in the other bed began to live for those one-hour periods where his world would be broadened and enlivened by all the activity and color of the world outside.

The window overlooked a park with a lovely lake. Ducks and swans played on the water while children sailed their model boats. Young couples walked arm in arm amidst flowers of every color and a fine view of the city skyline could be seen in the distance.

As the man by the window described all this in exquisite detail, the man on the other side of the room would close his eyes and imagine the picturesque scene.

One warm afternoon the man by the window described a parade passing by. Although the other man couldn't hear the band - he could see it. In his mind's eye as the gentleman by the window portrayed it with descriptive words.

Days and weeks passed. One morning, the nurse arrived to bring water for their baths only to find the lifeless body of the man by the window, who had died peacefully in his sleep. She was saddened and called the hospital attendants to take the body away.

As soon as it seemed appropriate, the other man asked if he could be moved next to the window. The nurse was happy to make the switch, and after making sure he *was comfortable, she left him alone.*

Slowly, painfully, he propped himself up on one elbow to take his first look at the real world outside. He strained to slowly turn to look out the window beside the bed. It faced a blank wall.

The man asked the nurse what could have compelled his deceased roommate who had described such wonderful things outside this window. The nurse responded that the man was blind and could not even see the wall. She said, "Perhaps he just wanted to encourage you."

Lessons:

There is tremendous happiness in making others happy, despite our own situations. Shared grief is half the sorrow, but happiness when shared, is doubled.
If you want to feel rich, just count all the things you have that money can't buy.
People will forget what you said . . .

People will forget what you did . . .

But people will never forget how you made them feel . . .
Make someone happy, share a kind word today.

"A good word is charity." (Bukhari & Muslim)

Have You Booked "The Most Inspirational Muslim Woman Speaker In America"?

Zohra Sarwari

The Ideal Professional Speaker for Your Next Event!

"Zohra Sarwari has a great skill for making you want to achieve on a higher level. Your students will enjoy learning from her!"

Jonathan Sprinkles
Former APCA National College 'Speaker of the Year'
<u>*www.jsprinkles.com*</u>

"After hearing Zohra Sarwari's speech, I was profoundly moved by her enthusiasm to further educate me on the way the Muslim's live. Her knowledge instilled a greater understanding and appreciation in me."

Debbie Burke
High School Teacher
Indianapolis, Indiana

Interested in other products by Zohra? Take a look at what she has to offer:

'9 Steps To Achieve Your Destiny'
Become The Change That You Envision In This World

'9 Steps To Achieve Your Destiny' *explores the steps that, if practiced daily, will change your life God-willing. It shows you how your thinking and habits can either make you successful or stagnant, and helps you navigate your way to the right choices and productive habits. At times each of us may find ourselves lost in the darkness, searching for answers. This book will guide you to the light and help you stay there.* **'9 Steps To Achieve Your Destiny'** *will open your eyes to your own untapped strengths that can steer you to personal success. Seeking knowledge is key. Let the journey begin!*

NO! I AM NOT A TERRORIST!

'Terrorism' and 'terrorist' are the latest media buzzwords! However, do you actually know what each of these terms mean? Do you know who a 'terrorist' is? What comes to your mind when you think of a 'terrorist'? Is it a man with a beard, or is it a woman in a veil? Muslims worldwide are being stereotyped and labeled as 'terrorists'. Have you ever stopped and wondered why? Have you ever made the time to discover what lies under the beard and the dress? Have you ever stopped to think what Islam actually has to say about 'terrorism'? Find the answers to all the above questions and more in this book, **'NO! I AM NOT A TERRORIST!'**

Are Muslim Women Oppressed?

Are Muslim Women
OPPRESSED?

ZOHRA SARWARI

Learn about the dignified and well-managed lives of Muslim women and know the reasons why they dress the way they do. **'Are Muslim Women OPPRESSED?'** *answers your questions: Why do Muslim women wear those weird clothes? Are they doing it for men? Are they inferior? Do they have no rights?* **'Are Muslim Women OPPRESSED?'** *will reveal the truth behind the concealed Muslim woman. It is a voyage from behind the veil to the real freedom and will give you an insight about Muslim women like you have never read before. Read and clear the misconceptions; separate the facts from the myths!*

Powerful Time Management Skills for Muslims

Islam holds Muslims responsible for every action they do and they will be held answerable for the things they are blessed with and how they used it. One of these blessings is 'Time'. **Powerful Time Management Skills for Muslims** *is explaining using references from the Quran and Sunnah how Muslims should live their lives and utilize the precious gift of 'Time'.*

Speaking Skills Every Muslim Must Know

Confidence is the key to success. **Speaking Skills Every Muslim Must Know** *shares with you some vital methods and techniques to develop confidence and helps you overcome your fear of public speaking. The book guides you following the pattern applied by the Prophet Muhammad(PBUH) and how he delivered his speeches.*

Time Management for Success
(e-book)

Become a Professional Speaker Today
(e-book)

Special Quantity Discount Offer!

- ► 20-99 books $13.00 per copy
- ► 100-499 books $10.00 each
- ► 500-999 books $7.00 each

LaVergne, TN USA
05 May 2010
181615LV00004B/2/P